Teacher's Handbook
of Classroom Programs
for Special Days

Teacher's Handbook of Classroom Programs for Special Days

Joseph C. DeVita

Philip Pumerantz

and

Ralph W. Galano

Parker Publishing Company, Inc.
West Nyack, N. Y.

© 1973, by

PARKER PUBLISHING COMPANY, INC.

West Nyack, N.Y.

Library of Congress Cataloging in Publication Data

DeVita, Joseph C.
   Teacher's handbook of classroom programs for special
days.

   Includes bibliographies.
   1. Schools--Exercises and recreations--United
States--Handbooks, manuals, etc. 2. Holidays--United
States. I. Pumerantz, Philip, joint author.
II. Galano, Ralph W.   joint author.
III. Title.
LB3525.D48   394.2'6'071073   72-13797
ISBN 0-13-888347-5

Printed in the United States of America

Dedication

for

Jeanne, Harriet, Peggy

ACKNOWLEDGMENT

The authors wish to acknowledge the assistance of numerous teachers throughout the country who suggested and tried out many of the ideas offered in this book. We are especially indebted to our colleagues at the university level and to our students there for their analyses and suggestions during the development of the manuscript.

Special appreciation goes to Mrs. Edith Launer of the Fairfield, Connecticut, Public Schools for contributing Chapter 12, "Chanukah and Passover"; to Mr. Gary Swenson of the Stamford, Connecticut, Public Schools for his assistance with Minority Groups in America in Chapter 10; to the pupils of the Fox Lane Middle School, Bedford, New York, for their assistance in implementing the materials suggested in the *American Studies* section; and finally to Dr. Morris Gall of Norwalk, Connecticut, for his advice and encouragement in beginning this book.

The Practical Value of This Book

You will find here a variety of activities that will help you enrich your classroom programs by utilizing holidays and special events in creative and innovative ways. The material in each chapter offers a break from the usual classroom routine, providing specific suggestions that will spark pupil participation, creativity, and planning. The broad range of activities includes ideas, materials, and methods that are suitable for teaching in any type of school, whether innovative or traditional in instruction and curriculum.

The emphasis is on practical approaches, and the work is organized according to selected holidays and special events that occur throughout the school year. Each chapter follows the general format of providing pertinent facts of value to the teacher, suggested classroom activities or lesson plans, and finally a bibliography with references to additional resource information. Material is also included that may be used as summer assignments for subsequent discussion and evaluation in the fall.

The book is divided into four principal sections: American Studies, Famous Americans, Ethnic Contributions, and International Themes. Increasingly, teachers are treating their everyday lessons from the standpoint of relevant themes or units rather than on the basis of individual, isolated topics. For example, Black History is treated in this book as a significant component of the section on Ethnic Contributions.

American education is facing increasingly challenging and critical issues. The problems confronting the existing schools and those that will emerge will be massive in scope and proportion.

With the public mandate to educate on a mass scale, teachers are hard pressed in terms of time, resources and know-how, to adequately meet the challenge. The pervasive and complex factors that are affecting and changing the nature of education have placed educators in the difficult position of trying to cope with the forces of change by employing better professional skills, supportive media, technology, and other effective innovations—all geared to the needs of today's students.

Ultimately, it is the *teacher* who determines the success or failure of American education. It is important then that the teaching role go beyond mere transmission of data; it must seek a broader function. It is essential that the creative capabilities of teachers be nourished and applied toward the greater use of more socially *relevant* material in the classroom. Readers will find the material in each of the following chapters to be particularly helpful in this respect.

Joseph C. DeVita
Philip Pumerantz
Ralph W. Galano

Table of Contents

Teacher's Handbook
of Classroom Programs
for Special Days

SECTION I
AMERICAN STUDIES

1

The Declaration of Independence
Independence Day

The Declaration of Independence is considered one of man's most eloquent documents. The draft was largely composed by Thomas Jefferson and a committee including John Adams, Benjamin Franklin, Robert Livingston, and Roger Sherman. It was perhaps, in the context of the time of its creation, a revolutionary document. The Declaration was, however, based upon many of the principles which had encouraged the revolution of 1688 in Great Britain.

The celebration of the adoption of the Declaration of Independence takes place on July 4, the date on which the Declaration was adopted by the representatives of the British Colonies in North America.

PERTINENT FACTS

1. In the spring of 1775 the delegates to the second Continental Congress assembled in Philadelphia, Pennsylvania, near a pleasant square which would later be known as Independence Square.
2. This fiercely independent group believed that mother England was denying them certain rights and privileges.
3. The first shots of revolution for independence were being fired at Lexington and Concord; however, perhaps it really started

with the ragged individuals who first settled back in Jamestown in 1607.

4. Just by location and time the foreign peoples who gathered in America were destined for self-government.

5. One of the first outrages occurred with the "writs of assistance," which allowed English officials to enter anyone's home without warning. James Otis in Boston in 1761 sounded the warning of things to come.

6. This was closely followed by Patrick Henry's declaration that the King had forfeited his right to obedience. This became known as the Parson's Cause and implied revolution.

7. In 1776 the Stamp Act, which required stamps to be affixed to all legal documents, newspapers, ship's papers, etc., sparked the slogan, "No taxation without representation."

8. The Stamp Act Congress met in New York with all thirteen colonies represented. The King repealed the Stamp Act, but the seeds were sown.

9. Charles Townshend pushed through the Townshend Act of 1767, which levied taxes on the importation of glass, paper, colors and tea, but after Sam Adams of Boston ignited the flames, the Parliament had to repeal the Act once again.

10. On December 6, 1773, a band of men disguised as Indians boarded a British tea ship in Boston Harbor and dumped the cargo into the water.

11. King George had Parliament pass the Coercive or Intolerable Acts to punish Massachusetts.

12. The Colonies banded together and the First Continental Congress took place in 1774 in Philadelphia.

13. Patrick Henry set the stage by his statement, "The distinctions between Virginians, Pennsylvanians, New Yorkers, and New Englanders are no more. I am not a Virginian, I am an American."

14. John Adams, a fire-eating radical, wrote, "We shall have nothing but deceit, hostility, fire, famine, pestilence and sword from administration and Parliament."

15. Thomas Paine's commonman's language made his pamphlet entitled *Common Sense* an influence throughout the Colonies.

Some excerpts attacked the divine rights of the King. Among the most potent were:

"A French bastard landed with an armed band, and established himself as King."

"One of the strongest proofs of the folly of hereditary rights in Kings, is that nature disapproves it, otherwise she would not so frequently turn it into ridicule by giving mankind an ass for a lion."

And his most important shot:

" 'Tis time to part."

16. The final blow came when the Parliament itself passed a search and seizure act against the Colonies' ships and cut off all trades. It was practically an act of war by the British.
17. Some of the most historical buildings depicting the Declaration of Independence are:
    a. Independence Hall, with a statue of Commodore John Barry in its front yard.
    b. Carpenters' Hall
    c. Pemberton House
18. A Liberty Bell Message: (This is the text for the taped message visitors hear at Independence Hall when they view the Liberty Bell.)

The Liberty Bell

You are looking at the Liberty Bell. Here is a symbol of law, of justice—a symbol of the sovereign rights of the people. This bell has played a greater role in history than any other bell in the world. Cracked and mute, resting silently here in the corridor of Independence Hall, it has been heard in the hearts of freedom-loving people throughout the world. Its effect as an emblem of liberty is magnetic, drawing those who seek their human birthright hopefully toward fulfillment.

But like the liberty it represents, the bell itself experienced many troubles and survived many problems. Each difficulty increased its value, and made it more enduring as a symbol. The bell was cast to commemorate the 50th Anniversary of William Penn's Charter of Privileges, a charter which insured freedom for the citizens of Pennsylvania. That was the reason for the prophetic Old Testament inscription "Proclaim liberty throughout all the land unto all the inhabitants thereof." A firm in England made the first cast in 1752, but the very first time it rang here in Philadelphia, it cracked. Not the crack you see here, for the 2,000 pound bell was recast from the same metal. The local workmen who remade the bell, we know only as Pass and Stow. They did their job well, for the bell rang for many years in the tower of this building. It called assemblymen to meetings, rang out the hours, rang as an alarm for fires; and since it quite probably rang for civic celebrations, we may assume that there were years following 1776 when it rang in observance of the 4th of July.

How did the crack you see here come about? Tradition has it that during the funeral procession for one of America's greatest men, it rang so steadily and with such force that it cracked. It was tolling the death of Chief Justice John Marshall, whose work on the United States Supreme Court did more than almost any man in preserving the Constitution of our country. Although an effort was made to save the tone of the bell by drilling the crack, this was not effective. An attempt was made to ring it again on George Washington's birthday. But the physical sound was dead. Thereafter, its symbolic message became more important than its actual ringing had ever been.

But the bell was not at first known as the Liberty Bell. It wasn't until a few years before the Civil War that opponents of slavery, heeding its inscription, "Proclaim Liberty," adopted the old bell as a symbol of their cause and called it the "Liberty Bell." Through poems, magazines and schoolbooks the bell soon became a universal symbol of liberty.

The Liberty Bell reminds each of us of our rights and privileges, but also our duties and responsibilities as free men. To each of us it suggests a rededication to the principles under which this country was founded. That is the silent, but forceful, and inspirational message of the Liberty Bell.

19. The first draft was written by Thomas Jefferson as a member of the Declaration Committee, which consisted of John Adams, Benjamin Franklin, Roger Sherman, and Robert Livingston.
20. Discuss the following questions and answers related to the Declaration of Independence:

The Declaration of Independence

One of our great American documents is the Declaration of Independence which was adopted by the Continental Congress in Philadelphia, July 4, 1776.

The Declaration of Independence charters our freedom as an independent nation among the "powers of the world." Thomas Jefferson, aided by such great Americans as John Adams and Benjamin Franklin, wrote the Declaration of Independence. Jefferson presented truths which form the principles of democratic government.

The Declaration of Independence states that all men are created equal and that God has given them the right to live, to be free, and to work for happiness. The duty of the government is to secure these rights for the people. The government, however, must get its power from the consent or agreement of the people governed.[1]

Questions and Answers on the Declaration of Independence:[2]

1. Q. When was the Declaration of Independence adopted? (Give day, month and year.)
   A. July 4, 1776.
2. Q. When did the members representing the thirteen states sign the Declaration?
   A. August 2, 1776.
3. Q. Name the thirteen states whose delegates signed the Declaration.

---

[1] *Know Your America,* prepared by the American Legion, Indianapolis, Indiana.

[2] Prepared by Mr. Floyd Haight, of Dearborn High School and a member of the Fort Dearborn Post No. 364, The American Legion, Dearborn, Michigan.

A. New Hampshire, Massachusetts Bay, Rhode Island, Connecticut, New York, New Jersey, Pennsylvania, Delaware, Maryland, Virginia, North Carolina, South Carolina and Georgia.

4. Q. Where is the original copy of the Declaration of Independence?

A. The original copy of the Declaration of Independence is kept in the National Archives Building in Washington, D. C. It was formerly displayed in the Library of Congress from 1921 to 1952.

5. Q. Name the president of the Congress which formulated the document.

A. John Hancock.

6. Q. Give the name of the person who drew up the Declaration of Independence.

A. Thomas Jefferson.

7. Q. Give the names of the committee members who were appointed to draw up a fitting Declaration of Independence.

A. Thomas Jefferson, Benjamin Franklin, John Adams, Roger Sherman, and Robert (R.) Livingston.

8. Q. How many of the colonies had voted to pass Lee's resolution for independence by July 2?

A. Twelve. (New York had not adopted it.)

9. Q. How many members of the Congress signed the Declaration of Independence?

A. Fifty-six.

10. Q. Is the original copy of the Declaration of Independence still displayed to the public?

A. Yes.

11. Q. How many arbitrary and tyrannical acts are listed in the Declaration?

A. Twenty-seven.

12. Q. What did the members signing the Declaration of Independence pledge to each other in the document?

A. Lives, fortunes, and sacred honor.

13. Q. Does the Declaration state that all men are "created equal" or "born equal"?

A. Created equal.

14. Q. What famous document embodied the statement not used in answer to question thirteen?
    A. The French "Rights of Man."
15. Q. Under what circumstances does the Declaration of Independence state that the people have a right to alter and abolish government?
    A. When the government fails to derive its power from consent of the governed.
16. Q. Does the Declaration state that governments should be changed because transient conditions change?
    A. No. (Should not be changed "for light and transient causes.")
17. Q. Are the words, "life, liberty and the pursuit of happiness," as mentioned in the Declaration of Independence, found in the Constitution of the United States?
    A. No. (The words, "life, liberty and pursuit of happiness," as mentioned in the Declaration of Independence are not found in the Constitution of the United States.)
18. Q. What specific rights and powers did the Declaration of Independence state that the new nation should have?
    A. "Levy war, conclude peace, contract alliances, and establish commerce (and do all other acts and things which independent states may of right do)."
19. Q. At what city was the Declaration of Independence first read to the army?
    A. New York.
20. Q. Are many of the arbitrary and tyrannical acts as listed in the Declaration of Independence mentioned in the Constitution which was adopted in 1788?
    A. No. (A large number of the arbitrary and tyrannical acts have been embodied in amendments to the Constitution. "Bill of Rights.")
21. Q. In the Declaration, it is stated that the right to rule comes from what source?
    A. The consent of the governed.
22. Q. Was the Declaration, as first drawn by Jefferson, changed by the committee?

A. Slightly. (The clause condemning the slave trade and another concerning the English people were struck out.)

23. Q. Did Jefferson write the Declaration without referring to books or other records?

A. Yes. (He said, "I turned to neither book nor pamphlet while writing it.")

24. Q. What was the name of the Congress that adopted the Declaration of Independence?

A. Second Continental Congress.

25. Q. The Congress that adopted the Declaration met in what city?

A. Philadelphia.

26. Q. Give date upon which the Congress convened.

A. May 10, 1775.

27. Q. Has the American government always followed the ideals of the Declaration of Independence?

A. No. (Two very good exceptions have occurred: First, the slave trade which obviously was contrary to the ideal of equality of man. John Calhoun, of South Carolina, during the slave period, said, "The chief obstruction in the way of the system was the constant reading of the Declaration of Independence." Second, the taking of foreign possessions against the consent of the governed.)

28. Q. The last paragraph of the Declaration practically restates the famous resolution made by what man?

A. (Richard Henry) Lee.

29. Q. Name the men who signed the Declaration of Independence and who later also signed the Constitution. Name the state from which each came.

A. Roger Sherman from Connecticut.
Benjamin Franklin from Pennsylvania.
Robert Morris from Pennsylvania.
George Clymer from Pennsylvania.
James Wilson from Pennsylvania.
George Read from Delaware.

LESSON PLANS

1. Conduct a simulated meeting; assign role playing parts of famous men involved. Parts should be assigned after famous men have been discussed and commented upon, as a result of specific research and reading. Each student might become an "authority" on the person he represents. The teacher will have to stimulate the dynamics of the group by presenting suggestions or questions at the appropriate time. The teacher must also remind students of the incident's place in the general sweep of history.

2. Have students write an invocation or commentary which could be presented in an assembly related to Independence Day. They could assume the role of a minister, political personage, student, etc.

3. Singing of patriotic songs.

4. Introduction and participation of guest speakers from veterans' groups or historical societies.

5. Selection of newspaper articles for discussions. Find the same topic from newspapers representing different points of view. Examine slant of news and reporting techniques.

6. Have students compose a position paper on the importance of celebrating this day. Assume a moderate, liberal, or conservative role. They might prepare this as an editorial for an assumed newspaper.

7. Creative and appropriate posters.

8. Forum or debates on pertinent topics.

9. Send for and review literature on the "Largest celebration in America during the Nation's birthday. Involving 20,000 local citizens." Provo L.D.S. Activities, Provo, Utah.

10. Send for *Know Your America,* published by the American Legion, National Headquarters, P.O. Box 1055, Indianapolis, Indiana 46206.

11. Consider official statements, positions or proclamations of various political leaders. A proclamation by a governor is a good example of an attitude or statement of position. Read

and discuss your state governor's proclamation, such as John Dempsey's of Connecticut:

State of Connecticut

[Seal]

By His Excellency JOHN DEMPSEY, Governor: a PROCLAMATION

Our nation pauses once again to celebrate the anniversary of the adoption and signing of a statement which a 33-year-old lawyer drafted in half a day's time, but which has become one of the most significant documents in world history.

The Declaration of Independence and its author, Thomas Jefferson, never will be forgotten. Nor will those courageous Americans who put their very lives in jeopardy by signing it, including Roger Sherman, Samuel Huntington, William Williams and Oliver Wolcott of Connecticut.

The action taken by the four Connecticut representatives and their 52 co-signers on July 4, 1776 served to strengthen the determination and the spirit of unity among the Colonies. It marked the beginning of a new nation, founded on principles of liberty and justice.

In accordance with the statutes of Connecticut, July 4 is observed each year as a holiday to remind our citizens of the significance of the Declaration of Independence, and to honor the memory of the Colonial leaders responsible for its adoption.

Therefore, I hereby proclaim Saturday, July 4, 1970, to be

INDEPENDENCE DAY

In connection with this important holiday, I call the attention of our citizens to the practice, revived in Connecticut after a lapse of almost a century and now observed throughout the country, of "ringing bells for freedom."

I urge full compliance with the resolution of the Connecticut General Assembly which calls for bells to be rung in churches and public buildings for four minutes, beginning at two o'clock in the afternoon on July 4.

It is fitting also, on this holiday, to take note of other special programs of observance such as "Operation Patriotism" sponsored by the Pennsylvania Society of the Sons of the American Revolution and the American Revival Society.

May all of our citizens, each in the manner that seems most fitting to him, make Independence Day, 1970, an occasion to re-affirm our faith in the principles for which our nation has stood since its founding 194 years ago.

[Seal of Connecticut] Given under my hand and seal of the State at the Capitol, in Hartford, this sixteenth day of June, in the year of our Lord one thousand nine hundred and seventy and of the Independence of the United States the one hundred and ninety-fourth.

/s/ John Dempsey

By His Excellency's Command:

/s/ Ella T. Grasso
Secretary of the State

BIBLIOGRAPHY AND RESOURCE MATERIALS

Becker, Carl L. *The Declaration of Independence*. New York: Alfred A. Knopf, 1942.

Boyd, Julian P. *The Declaration of Independence: The Evolution of the Text*. Washington, D. C.: Library of Congress, 1943.

Burnett, Edmund C. *The Continental Congress*. New York: Macmillan Co., 1941.

Commager, Henry S. and Morris, R. B. *Spirit of Seventy-Six: The Story of the American Revolution As Told by Participants*. Indianapolis: Bobbs-Merrill, 1958.

Eberlein and Hubbard. *Diary of Independence Hall*. Philadelphia: J. B. Lippincott Co., 1948.

Fitzpatrick, John C. *The Spirit of the Revolution*. New York: Houghton-Mifflin Co., 1924.

Hazelton, John H. *The Declaration of Independence: Its History*. New York: Dodd-Mead & Co., 1906.

Malone, Milhollen, and Kaplan. *The Story of the Declaration of Independence*. New York: Oxford University Press, 1954.

Mearns, David C. *The Declaration of Independence: The Story of a Parchment*. Washington, D.C.: U.S. Government Printing Office, 1950.

Muller, John C. *Origins of the American Revolution*. Boston: Little, Brown and Co., 1943.

Moore, Frank. *The Diary of the American Revolution*. New York: Charles Scribners, 1860.

Smith, Page. *John Adams*. New York: Doubleday and Co., 1962.

2
Flag Day

The study of the development and significance of flags (vexillology) can provide an interesting dimension to the social studies program. The specific celebration of Flag Day honors the American Flag and the principles that it represents. President Woodrow Wilson established Flag Day in a proclamation issued on May 30, 1916.

The American flag has recently become a symbol for and against the many controversies existing between groups who either agree or disagree with various government policies. It is now essential that students be given an opportunity to objectively review the history and significance of the nation's flag. Its use has recently been the subject of considerable legal action and discussion. Portions of a recent newspaper article provide a good example:

Flag Misuse Disputes Await Supreme Court

Washington *(AP)*—The Supreme Court is headed into an emotional controversy over the American flag.

Two appeals from New York awaiting the justices' return next month provide pivotal tests of efforts to shield the flag from scorn or even use by radicals.

Historically, the flag has been an object of veneration for fervent patriots. But it's also been used as a political banner, as a call to arms, a symbol of injustice and as a target of mockery.

The question confronting the court is whether Americans

can be sent to prison because of the way they use the flag.

In one case, the owner of a Madison Avenue art gallery was convicted for exhibiting seven constructions by an artist and war protester.

In the second case, four Long Island women and two organizations opposed to the Vietnam war have been threatened with prosecution for superimposing the traditional peace symbol upon a representation of the flag. Arrests for displaying the emblem are common in New York City.

Last year, the Supreme Court ruled 5 to 4 that the Constitution protects those who denounce the flag in words. The decision reversed the conviction of a Brooklyn bus driver who burned a flag in outrage after hearing a civil rights activist had been ambushed and shot.

The court avoided, however, the issue of whether people can be punished for burning or defacing the American flag.

A defendant contends New York state's 1967 flag desecration law violates the First Amendment's free speech guarantee. He argues respect for the flag cannot be compelled in a free society.

The New York Court of Appeals disagreed in upholding his conviction on a 5-2 vote. The majority noted that "insults to a flag have been the cause of war," and said the defendant cannot cast contempt upon the flag to express his views.

The Long Island war protesters are attacking another New York law, one that forbids placing any word, design or drawing upon the flag, whatever the purpose. This, they say, is an unconstitutional attempt to compel respect for the flag.

"In a free society no person should be compelled to make ritualistic obeisance to a trapping of the state, whether by being forced to salute it or by being forced to treat it as though it were the secular equivalent of a religious icon," their appeal says.

Last June, a federal court in New York City said the law could not be applied to the peace emblem because it was not a flag in a legal sense. But the court said the law's prohibition against using the flag as a design did not violate the Constitution.

All the states and the federal government have laws that

forbid the desecration of the flag. Their validity is at stake in the two appeals.[1]

PERTINENT FACTS [2]

1. The very first flag planted on the North American continent was the Viking flag. It was brought here by Leif Ericson and his Norse explorers.
2. In 1492 Christopher Columbus brought the Royal Standard of Spain.
3. The Red Cross of St. George, England's universal banner until 1606, was carried to our shores by John Cabot in 1497.
4. The Fleur-de-lis of France was the flag under which Jacques Cartier explored the northern half of the continent in the mid-1500's.
5. In 1626, after Henry Hudson bought Manhattan Island from the Indians for twenty-four dollars' worth of trinkets, the flag of the Netherlands was raised over the new colony.
6. From 1638 to 1655, the Swedish flag flew in Delaware.
7. In 1687, when New England, New York and New Jersey were unified under English rule, the Andros flag flew high.[3]
8. The Union Jack, a consolidation of the English and Scottish flags, was the banner under which the colonies were formed.
9. Finally, in 1707, a new flag of Great Britain, the British Red Ensign, was raised over the colonies. This was the flag the British troops carried during the Revolutionary War.
10. Other flags began to appear as signs of revolution:
    a. The Endicott Flag, fashioned by John Endicott of Salem, Mass.
    b. The Gadsden Flag, one of many rattlesnake flags, demonstrated the settlers' extreme resentment of British rule.

---

[1] *The Stamford* [Conn.] *Advocate* (Associated Press), September 18, 1970.
[2] *Pertinent Facts*—contributed by S. P. Wright and Company, Springfield, Ill., 1970.
[3] Sir Edmund Andros was the English governor of American colonies.

    c. The Green Tree Flag was a favorite emblem in Massachusetts.

    d. The Liberty Tree Flag was the identifying emblem of the Sons of Liberty who planned the Boston Tea Party in 1773.

    e. The flag of Bunker Hill, where Colonel William Prescott fought the first major engagement of the American Revolution. This is where he stated the immortal phrase, "Don't fire until you see the whites of their eyes!"

11. The Grand Union Flag was officially adopted by the Continental Congress in 1775.

12. "Old Glory" . . .

    It was on June 14, 1777, that the Continental Congress adopted a design for the first national flag.

    At that time, it was resolved that "The flag of the United States shall be thirteen stripes, alternate red and white, with a union of thirteen stars of white on a blue field, representing a new constellation."

    The only difference between this and the Grand Union Flag was that the former replaced the crosses of England and Scotland with a circle of stars.

    "Old Glory" remained unchanged from 1777 until January 13, 1794. Congress then voted to add two stripes and two stars, in recognition of the admission of Vermont and Kentucky.

    By 1818, there were a total of twenty states, so Congress voted in April of that year to standardize the flag. It was to have thirteen alternate red and white stripes, symbolizing the original thirteen states. A star was to be added to the blue field for each new state, on the July 4 following admission.

    This rule has remained in effect, bringing the flag up to its present 50-star status.

13. In procession with several other flags, the United States flag should be on the military right of line.

14. In procession with several other flags, the United States flag should be in front of the center of the other flags.

15. When with other flags on the same halyard, the United States flag should be on top.
16. With two or more flags in line, the United States flag should be at the right of all other flags.
17. With another flag on the wall, the United States flagstaff should be in front of the other flag.
18. With a group of flags, the United States flag should be in the center and above all others.
19. On a staff projecting from a building, the union of the United States flag should be at the peak of the staff.
20. From a rope over a sidewalk, the union of the United States flag should be away from the building.
21. Hanging staffless, the United States flag's union should be uppermost and to the viewer's left.
22. Over the center of a public street, the United States flag should hang vertically with the union to the north (in an east-west street) or to the east (in a north-south street).
23. On a speaker's platform, displayed on a staff, the United States flag should occupy the position of honor on the speaker's right.
24. On a speaker's platform, displayed flat the United States flag should be above and beyond the speaker.
25. When to display the flag—Section 2 of the federal flag code states that:

It is the universal custom to display the flag only from sunrise to sunset on buildings and stationary flagstaffs in the open. However, the flag may be displayed at night upon special occasions when it is desired to produce a patriotic effect.

It should also be displayed on all days when the weather permits, especially on New Year's Day, January 1; Inauguration Day, January 20; Lincoln's Birthday, February 12; Washington's Birthday, February 22; Armed Forces Day, third Saturday in May; Easter Sunday; Mother's Day, second Sunday in May; Memorial Day (half staff until noon), May 30; Flag Day, June 14; Independence Day, July 4; Labor Day, first Monday in September; Constitution Day, September 17; Columbus Day, October 12; Veterans Day, November 11; Thanksgiving Day, fourth Thursday in November; Christmas Day, December 25; such other days as may be proclaimed by the President of the United States; the birthdays of the States; and on State holidays.

The flag should be displayed daily, weather permitting, on or near the main administration building of every public institution . . . every polling place on election days . . . and during school days in or near every schoolhouse.

LESSON PLANS

1. The Teacher's Edition of Scholastic *Scope,* September 14, 1970, has devoted pages 2–7 to "Whose Flag?" It is at least thought-provoking and is designed to fire up discussion, understanding, and encourage further study of our flag. It is quoted here with the permission of the publisher.

Whose Flag?

The Flag, a Symbol of Patriotism

The flag is one of the symbols or signs of patriotism. So many flags are being shown today that some people say patriotism is stronger than ever. But others are worried. They say the flag is being used—and misused—in ways that divide Americans, instead of joining them.

Flags have become so popular that flag makers cannot keep up with orders. Flag stickers are also popular. A magazine sent out 20 million flag stickers last year. A chain of gas stations gave away 20 million, too. A men's club gave out millions more.

They are pasted on stores, houses, luggage, fences, cars, trucks, bikes. Some have words printed on them, like:

"America—love it or leave it."
"If your heart isn't in it, get out."

Many men and women are wearing flag pins on their clothes. Thousands of policemen wear them on their uniforms. A supermarket in Atlanta offered a flag pin with every five-dollar purchase. A pizza shop in Michigan gave away little flags to those who bought their pies. Many businesses are using the flag in advertisements.

Other businessmen are selling star-spangled ashtrays, jewelry, pens, beer mugs. Some people wear shirts or ties showing parts of the American flag. One actress has a bedspread with stars and stripes on it.

For people who are against the war in Viet Nam, there are flags with a peace symbol in place of the stars. And there are stickers with the flag printed over a dove. There are also flag pins and stickers with words printed on them, like:

"Peace now. Get out of Viet Nam."
"Give peace a chance."

Other stickers are for people who support unity between blacks and whites. These show the flag held in two hands— one black and one white.

In 1942, Congress passed some "rules and customs" for showing the flag. They say the flag should not be shown on a car, "except from a staff." It should "never have placed on it any word, design, or drawing." It should not be used as part of "a costume." It should "never be carried flat, but always aloft and free." But Congress did not say what should be done if people break these rules.

Which of these uses of the flag do you approve of? Which are you against? Do any seem to break the "rules and customs" for showing the flag? If so, what do you think should be done in such cases?

What Does the Flag Mean?

The flag means different things to different people. For example:

"To tell you why I love and respect the flag so much would take a book. It would be the long, brave story of America. Briefly, I love our flag because it is the most beautiful national banner of all. It stands today, as always, for the finest nation on earth."

—Dwight D. Eisenhower

"I wouldn't fly the flag on the Fourth of July or any other day. When I see a car with a flag pasted on it, I figure the guy behind the wheel isn't my friend. Most flag-wavers are either for the war in Viet Nam or against minorities—or both."

—Jackie Robinson

"You can call me a flag-waver any time you want to. I think that's something to be proud of. A flag-waver is proud of his country. I think of all the people that died for that flag. If somebody's going to spit on it, it's like spitting on their grave. So they better not spit on it in front of me. You think you could have it better some place else? Well, then, don't hang around here. Go there."

—A building worker

"A flag is a piece of cloth. It's what it stands for that counts. Burning it is like burning the bad things it stands for now—My Lai, racial injustice, shooting students. It doesn't have anything to do with the goodness of America."

—A flag burner

"What does the flag mean to me? Everything I've gotten in this country. It means my children. It means everything. If it was my own son, I'd kill him if he destroyed the flag."

—A construction worker

"I told the children we would not be getting the flag out for Flag Day this year. When I was a kid during the Second World War, the flag stood for something decent and kind. Now it stands for something very different. How do you tell children how that can happen?"

—A father

"I display the flag to show I love my country. That doesn't mean I like this war. It doesn't mean I like everything our government does. But when your country is in a war and is being criticized, you must show you stand behind it."

—A mother

"Sure, I carried an American flag in the last peace march. But it was the one with 13 stars. It was the flag of the Declaration of Independence. It says that all men are created equal and that all have a right to life and liberty. Many people who are showing the flag today are using it for other reasons. They're showing they're against people who protest this unjust war. They stand for death, not life. They're not for liberty, because they want to beat or jail or kill those who think differently."

—A peace demonstrator

"Some of these flag-users hate everything that's young. They think the National Guardsmen who shot students at Kent State deserve a medal. In many ways, they are like the Germans Hitler turned into Nazis. They carry this flag thing to an extreme. . . . Still, I have to admit that the American flag gives me a chill when it goes by. I don't want to knock it. I saw some good men bleed and die for it during World War II. It stood for good dreams once. I think it can again. I don't think the kids appreciate what the flag meant to people."

—A longshoreman

"I don't think anybody loves the flag more than some of the people who are against the war."

—Billy Graham

"Why shouldn't blacks, young people—any minority group—fly any flag they like? There are people in the South who have flown the Confederate flag for years. No one suggested they be punished for it."

—A professor

"Our respect is not to the flag as a piece of cloth. It is to what the flag means in our lives. It is to the land, the persons, the laws, the ideals that the flag stands for. . . . May our flag forever remain the symbol of a nation dedicated to freedom, justice, and the well-being of all mankind."

—John Williams Kaplan

How do you feel when you see the flag? Which of these views is most like your own? Which is most unlike your view?

Which loyalty is most important to you? To country? To conscience or ideals? To family? To friends? To race? To religion? To mankind? Write a statement indicating your response to some of the above questions.

2. Read and evaluate the following proclamation of the Governor of Connecticut:

STATE OF CONNECTICUT

[Seal]

By His Excellency JOHN DEMPSEY, Governor: a

PROCLAMATION

One hundred and ninety-three years ago, representatives from thirteen states, resolutely dedicated to the principles of freedom and justice, met in Philadelphia on June 14 and approved a design for a national flag.

Chosen as a symbol of the spirit and determination of a vigorous new nation, struggling against overwhelming odds to establish its independence, the flag consisted of thirteen alternate red and white stripes and thirteen stars on a field of blue.

In 1795, with the admission of Vermont and Kentucky to the Union, two stripes and stars were added to the flag. As our nation expanded, however, it soon became apparent that it was impractical to continue to add new stripes. In 1818, design of the flag, by direction of Congress, reverted to the 13 stripes representing the original states, with one star for each state and provision for addition of new stars as needed.

The flag of the United States, flown proudly at home and as a source of inspiration to our fighting men in distant parts of the world, has ever been regarded with respect by all responsible citizens. A reminder of our heritage, it is deserving of honor and our unswerving allegiance.

To mark the anniversary of the adoption of the flag by

the United States I proclaim, in accordance with the statutes of our state, Sunday, June 14, to be

FLAG DAY

I urge that as this day approaches, special Flag Day exercises be held in our schools so that students may have the opportunity to acquire a full understanding of the significance of the Stars and Stripes and all that they represent.

I urge also, in observance of this occasion, that the flag be displayed on homes and public buildings and that appropriate commemorative exercises be conducted in communities throughout Connecticut.

[Seal of Connecticut]
Given under my hand and seal of the State at the Capitol, in Hartford, this third day of June, in the year of our Lord one thousand nine hundred and seventy and of the Independence of the United States the one hundred and ninety-fourth.

/s/   John Dempsey

By His Excellency's Command:

/s/ Ella T. Grasso
Secretary of the State

3. Follow Proclamation with appropriate classroom discussions, grouping by small groups and individual assignments.
4. The following course of study is contributed by the American Legion, the National Americanism Commission, Indianapolis, Indiana 46204 in their publication, *Know Your America*. Certain sections are quoted here:

1. Q. By what authority was our first National Flag established?
   A. Authorized by the Continental Congress.
2. Q. Quote the exact language of the original Flag law.
   A. Resolved, That the Flag of the United States be thirteen stripes, alternate red and white; that the union

be thirteen stars, white in a blue field, representing a new constellation.

3. Q. When was our state first represented by a star in the union of the National Flag?

  A. _____ (Answers to be inserted to apply to your particular state.)

4. Q. Name the original states represented by the stripes of the Flag.

  A. New Hampshire, Massachusetts, Connecticut, Rhode Island, New York, Delaware, Pennsylvania, Maryland, Virginia, North Carolina, South Carolina, Georgia and New Jersey.

5. Q. When was the first law passed that governs the present design of the Flag?

  A. April 4, 1818.

6. Q. Mention two early American Flags which suggested part of the design of the present Flag.

  A. Naval ensign 1776–1777. Striped union 1776–1777.

7. Q. What was the official Flag of the United States between September 3, 1777, and January 13, 1794? Between May 1, 1795, and April 4, 1818?

  A. Flag of 13 stars and 13 stripes. Flag of 15 stars and 15 stripes.

8. Q. When it arises from the ground or a low foundation, what should be the approximate length of a Flag pole, expressed in lengths of a Flag displayed?

  A. Col. Kerrick, in his authoritative book, *The Flag of the United States,* says: "To secure best effect and appearance, a Flag pole, in height above the ground, should be three or four times the length of the Flag to be displayed."

9. Q. Mention four contemporary Flag designs, other than the Stars and Stripes, which have been established by Congress.

  A. Yacht ensign, Revenue Flag, President's Flag, Navy Union Jack.

10. Q. What date do we observe as the anniversary of the Flag? When and by whom was this anniversary proclaimed?

  A. June 14. President Wilson, 1915.

11. Q. According to a statement ascribed to George Washington, what is the significance of each of the colors in the Flag?

    A. We take the stars and blue union from Heaven, the red from our Mother Country, separating it by white stripes, thus showing that we have separated from her, and the white stripes shall go down to posterity representing liberty.

12. Q. What was the inscription on the Pine Tree Flag? On the Rattlesnake Flag? In what colony did each of these Flags originate?

    A. "An Appeal to Heaven," "Don't Tread on Me," Massachusetts and North Carolina.

13. Q. What are the proportions of the National Flag?

    A. Width, 1; length 1.9; width of union, 7/13; length of union, 0.76; width of each stripe, 1/13; diameter of each star, .0616.

14. Q. When and by whom were the present proportions established?

    A. President Taft, 1912; revoked and republished by President Wilson, 1916.

15. Q. On what days should the Flag be displayed?

    A. On all days of patriotic observance and on the occasion of visits from high government officials. Schools and public buildings should display it every day.

16. Q. What naval commander first flew the Stars and Stripes? When and over what ship?

    A. John Paul Jones. *Ranger,* July 8, 1777.

17. Q. What is the proper salute to the Flag by a man or boy in civilian clothes? By a woman or girl?

    A. Remove hat and hold it at the left shoulder with right hand over the heart. Right hand over the heart.

18. Q. What is our National Anthem? By whom was it written? Under what conditions?

    A. "The Star-Spangled Banner," Francis Scott Key. Written while a captive of the British during a night attack on Fort McHenry, September 13, 1814.

19. Q. How is the Flag displayed on Memorial Day?

    A. Half-mast until noon, then raised to full staff until sunset.

20. Q. When the Flag becomes faded, frayed or otherwise damaged, how should it be disposed of?

A. It should be destroyed privately, preferably by burning, or some other method in harmony with reverence and respect we owe to the emblem representing our country.

21. Q. During what part of the day should the Flag be displayed when it is flown from a halyard?

A. Sunrise to sunset.

22. Q. Who gave the name of "Old Glory" to the Flag?

A. Capt. William Driver.

23. Q. Is the Flag of the United States ever dipped in salute to any individual?

A. No.

24. Q. How may the Flag be used in connection with the unveiling of a monument?

A. It should never be used to cover the statue, but should be flung aloft to the right of it.

25. Q. Is it correct to use the Flag for a merely decorative purpose in any printed, painted or embroidered design?

A. No.

26. Q. When the Flag is suspended from a cord or wire over the center of a street, what should be the position of the union?

A. The union should be to the north in an east and west street or to the east in a north and south street.

27. Q. Describe the Striped Union Flag.

A. Thirteen horizontal stripes alternate red and white with the English union cantoned in the corner.

28. Q. How is crepe used with the Flag to indicate mourning? By whose order?

A. On the flagstaff by attaching two streamers of black crepe to the spearhead. By order of the President.

29. Q. Should the Flag be worn as a part of any costume or uniform?

A. No.

30. Q. In what war did the Stars and Stripes first replace regimental colors as the official Flag of the Army of the United States?

A. Mexican War in 1846–47.

31. Q. What is the meaning of a Flag flown with the union down?
    A. Sign of distress.

32. Q. Describe the coat-of-arms of the United States.
    A. Chief figure of an American eagle holding an olive branch in his right talon and a bundle of thirteen arrows in his left. Superimposed on him is a blue shield bearing thirteen vertical stripes, alternate red and white with a plain blue chief. In the beak of the eagle is a scroll with the motto: E Pluribus Unum.

33. Q. Should a Flag be hoisted rapidly, or slowly and ceremoniously? How should it be lowered?
    A. Rapidly. Slowly and ceremoniously.

34. Q. Quote the pledge of allegiance to the Flag.
    A. "I pledge allegiance to the Flag of the United States of America and to the Republic for which it stands, one Nation under God, indivisible, with liberty and justice for all."

35. Q. How is the pledge of allegiance to the Flag given?
    A. Standing, with right hand over heart. The position to be held to the end.

36. Q. When used to cover the casket of a veteran, what should be the position of the union of the Flag?
    A. Union of the Flag is placed over left shoulder of the body.

37. Q. At what position in a parade should the Flag of the United States be carried?
    A. In front and at the right of a column or section. If other flags are carried it may go before them at center of line.

38. Q. Was the Flag of the United States flown over the front line troops during the First World War? Over what occupied territory was it flown after the Armistice?
    A. No. Germany.

39. Q. What should be done by all spectators while the Flag of the United States is being hoisted or lowered?
    A. They should stand at attention, the men uncovering.

40. Q. How is a Flag correctly displayed on an automobile?

A. Fix it to a staff at the radiator cap. Do not drape.

41. Q. When a Flag is displayed flat against a wall, what should be the position of the union?

A. The union should always be at the observer's left.

42. Q. Should the Flag be lowered into a grave?

A. No.

43. Q. Since the passage of the National Flag resolve, what Presidents have issued orders affecting the proportions of the Flag.

A. Presidents Monroe, Taft and Wilson.

44. Q. What is the correct position for the mounted Flag on a speaker's platform?

A. At the speaker's right.

45. Q. When was the first National Flag Conference called? By what organization? Who was the first speaker?

A. June 14, 1923. The American Legion. President Harding.

46. Q. Is it proper to drape or festoon the Flag?

A. No.

47. Q. Should portions of the air of "The Star-Spangled Banner" be interpolated in any medley?

A. No.

48. Q. When was the Flag of the United States first borne into a major engagement by the American Army?

A. Battle of Brandywine, September 7, 1777.

49. Q. Is it correct to place any object or emblem on or above the Flag of the United States?

A. No.

50. Q. What authority is there for the use of a yellow fringe on the Flag?

A. Authorized by U. S. Army Regulations as published by the War Department in 1923.

The following reference texts will supply the necessary information for the course of study outlined:

The Flag Code—National Americanism Commission, The American Legion, Indianapolis, Indiana.

Let's Be Right on Flag Etiquette—National Americanism Commission, Indianapolis, Indiana.

Origin and History of the Flag—George Henry Preble, Published by Frank-Maurice, Inc., 114 E. 32nd Street, New York, N.Y.

The Flag of the United States: Your Flag and Mine—Colonel Harrison S. Kerrick. Published by the White House, Chicago, Ill.

The Flag of the United States: Its History and Symbolism—Colonel James A. Moss. Published by the United States Flag Association, Washington, D. C.

How the Flag Became Old Glory—E. L. Scott. Published by the Macmillan Company, 60 Fifth Avenue, New York City.

BIBLIOGRAPHY AND RESOURCE MATERIALS

Aikman, Lonnelle. "New Stars for Old Glory." *National Geographic Magazine,* Vol. 116, No. 1 (July, 1959).

Boutell's Heraldry. Revised by C. W. Scott-Giles, M.A. London: Frederick Warne & Co., Ltd.

Brown's Flags and Funnels. London: Brown Son & Ferguson.

Brown's Signalling. London: Brown Son & Ferguson.

Chapin, Howard. *The Artistic Motives in the United States Flag.* Providence: Pavillon Club, 1930.

Chapin, Howard. "Colonial Military Flags." *The New England Quarterly,* Vol. IV, No. 3 (1931).

Chapin, Howard. *The New England Flag.* Providence: Pavillon Club, 1930.

Cumberland, Barlow. *History of the Union Jack.* Toronto: Briggs, 1911.

Cutler, Alfred Morton. *The Continental "Great Union" Flag.* Somerville, Mass.: School Committee, 1929.

Davis, Gherardi. *Regimental Colors in the War of the Revolution.* New York: Gilliss, 1907.

Edwards, Maj. T. J., M.B.E. F.R.Hist.S., *Regimental Colours.* London: Gale & Polden, Ltd.

Eggenberger, David. *Flags of the U.S.A.* New York: Crowell, 1964.

The Flag Bulletin. This quarterly journal has been published since 1961 by the Flag Research Center, 17 Farmcrest Avenue, Lexington, Mass. 02173. It contains articles on all kinds and aspects of flags, including flags of the United States.

Perrin, W. G. *British Flags.* Cambridge: Cambridge University Press, 1922.

Preble, George Henry. *History of the Flag of the United States.* Boston: Houghton, Mifflin, 1894.

Quaife, Milo M. *The Flag of the United States.* New York: Grosset and Dunlap, 1942.

Quaife, Milo M., *et al. The History of the United States Flag.* New York: Harper, 1961.

Spargo, John. *The Stars and Stripes in 1777.* Bennington, Vermont: Bennington Battle Monument and Historical Association, 1928.

The authors call special attention to the following text:

Smith, Whitney. *The Flag Book of the United States.* New York: William Morrow & Co., 1970.

3

Veterans Day

Veterans Day honors the men and women who have served in the Armed Forces of the United States. November 11 was designated as Armistice Day by Great Britain, France, and the United States, after World War I. Canada observes Remembrance Day on this date. In 1954 Congress changed the title to Veterans Day, in honor of the veterans of all wars, and, beginning in 1971, celebration of Veterans Day occurs on the fourth Monday in October.

This brief chapter provides some specific activities that pay tribute to the men and women who have served their country in all wars.

PERTINENT FACTS

1. World War I ended in 1918 at the 11th hour of the 11th day of the 11th month (November 11). The United States had been in the war since April 6, 1917—a little more than a year and a half. During this time, four million American men were in uniform; over 300,000 casualties were suffered; over 130,000 were killed.
2. In 1919 President Woodrow Wilson proclaimed November 11 as Armistice Day. In his proclamation he said:

> To us in America the reflections of Armistice Day will be filled with solemn pride in the heroism of those who died in the country's service and with gratitude for the victory, both

because of the opportunity it has given America to show her sympathy with peace and justice in the councils of the nations.

3. In 1921 the body of an unknown American soldier was brought from France and, on Armistice Day, buried in Arlington National Cemetery, Arlington, Virginia with elaborate ceremonies, including a parade from the National Capitol across the Potomac River to the cemetery. Each year since then, special services have been held at the Tomb of the Unknown Soldier on November 11, at 11:00 A.M.
4. Congress, in 1926, directed the President to issue an annual proclamation calling upon the people to observe the day.
5. During World War II, in which the United States was at war from December 7, 1941 to August 14, 1945, over one million casualties, including 400,000 killed, were suffered. Over fifteen million men and women served in the armed forces, and more than $200 billion was spent in winning the war.
6. In the Korean War, which lasted from June 25, 1950 to July 27, 1953, almost six million Americans served in the armed forces. The United States suffered 157,530 casualties, including almost 55,000 killed.
7. Closely paralleling the Korean conflict, the war in Vietnam also resulted in the sacrifice of over 40,000 American lives.
8. In 1954 Congress designated November 11 as Veterans Day to honor all American veterans.

LESSON PLANS

1. Have students report on the history of Veterans Day.
2. Students could cover and report on parades or special events that are occurring either locally or in places of national interest.
3. Interview officers of the local veterans organization.
4. Have students prepare news releases that may depict historical events pertinent to Veterans Day.
5. Bring in and report on medals, honors, discharges, souvenirs, and items their fathers, mothers, uncles, brothers, etc., may have earned.

6. Analyze the music and art of a particular war period.
7. Analyze the political cartoons pertaining to Veterans Day or a particular war period.
8. Develop local veteran bulletin boards.
9. Conduct panels or debates on the meaning and purpose of Veterans Day.
10. Have students relate some stories about their own families' service to our country.
11. Make up songs, poems and stories appropriate for the day or time period.

BIBLIOGRAPHY AND RESOURCE MATERIALS

Plays

In the Emperor's Garden, by Marion Holbrook
The Robber, by Grace H. Swift
Peace Pageant, by Hazel Carter Maxon

Poems

"War," by Dana Burnet
"The Illusion of War," by Richard LaGallienne
"War Time," by Isabel Fiske Conant
"Farragut," by William Tuckey Meredith
"Dulce Et Decorum Est," by Wilfred Owen
"Hit," by Rober Haven Schauffler
"This Is Not the Time," by Mac Flecknoe
"Armistice Miracle," by Isabel Fiske Conant
"Victory Bells," by Grace Hazard Conkling
"Armistice Day," by Mary Caroline Davies
"First Armistice Anniversary," by Isabel Fiske Conant
"The Gods of War," by George Russell (A.E.)
"Young Man Death," by Margaret Lathrop Law
"The English Graves," by Gilbert K. Chesterton
"Violet for a Stone," by Isabel Fiske Conant
"Psalm Forty-Six," by Robert Haven Schauffler
"A Word," by Gilbert K. Chesterton
"Let Us Have Peace," by Nancy Byrd Turner
"Two Sonnets for Eternal Armistice," (1931) by Ernest Hartsock
"In Salutation to the Eternal Peace," by Sarojini Naidu
"War Relics," by Tertius Van Dyke
"From Sonnets Written in the Fall of 1914," by George Edward Wood-
   berry
"Brotherhood," by Edwin Markham
"The Unborn of Your Dead," by Maxwell W. Allen
"After Armistice Day," by Isabel Fiske Conant
"New Earth," by Carrie Ward Lyon
"God's Eye View," by Robert Haven Schauffler

Editorials

"The Last Armistice and Its Lessons for the Next One," by William
  Philip Simms
"Unknown," by Bruce Barton
"Discussion of the Pledge of Allegiance"
"Reading of 'In Flander's Field' "

4

Memorial Day
May 30th

As a national holiday, Memorial Day is the observance of all the dead of all wars the United States of America has ever been engaged in.

Although wars are unpopular topics, and sometimes special days associated with wars are met with counterdemonstrations by antiwar groups, Memorial Day has pretty much escaped this type of reaction. It is a day of parades; a day of Scouts marching, of school bands, of Indian guide tribes, of fire departments, service clubs and volunteer agencies such as the Red Cross, teaming together to bring a day to remember for the local community. Certainly this day must have an educational place in the classrooms of our schools. The following pages are designed to meet this need.

PERTINENT FACTS

Origin of Memorial Day

1. Began as a gesture by some Southern women during the Civil War period who decorated graves of both Union and Confederate soldiers buried on Southern soil.
2. During this period of time it became known as Decoration Day. The graves were decorated with flowers during the month of May.
3. Major General John A. Logan in 1868 officially named May 30 as the special day for honoring the graves of Union soldiers.

4. Most of the Southern states have their own days for honoring the Confederate dead.
   April 26   Alabama, Florida, Georgia and Mississippi
   May 10   North Carolina and South Carolina
   June 3   Kentucky, Louisiana and Tennessee
5. Easton, Pennsylvania, also honors naval dead by setting afloat tiny ships filled with flowers.
6. Now observance also includes the dead of the Spanish-American War, World Wars I and II, the Korean War, and the Vietnamese War.
7. National celebrations handled by American Legion after World War I.
8. It is a legal holiday in most states.

Significance

1. Reminds us of presence of war and need for peace.
2. Stresses dignity of man and human worth.
3. Observes patriotism of American armed servicemen.

SUGGESTED CLASSROOM ACTIVITIES

Consider some of the following activities in which to involve your class as you pursue the study of Memorial Day:

1. Bulletin Board display consisting of pictures of Arlington Cemetery, Gettysburg Address, previous Memorial Day parades and ceremonies that might have been in the newspaper.
2. Encourage discussion of what wars do to people who fight, how they start, what they do to innocent people and what could be done to prevent them. Good social studies material.
3. Incorporate literature and library with poetry readings that express the feelings of war. Encourage students to compose their own as they begin to verbalize understandings.
4. Language arts essays on need for peace.
5. Map work using those states that celebrate different Memorial Days. Perhaps write letter to Chamber of Commerce about

naval observance in Easton, Pa. Language arts would incorporate need for correct salutation and structure of letter.

6. Since many youngsters will march in a parade with Scouts or other organizations, a committee could be set up to research who will handle the arrangements for the town, what the parade route will be, and who will be speaking. They could draw parade route on a large map, which could be the center of their own bulletin board.

7. Previous newspaper articles or essays and editorials might be researched and then the class as a whole might compose an editorial to be submitted to the local newspaper on the subject of the meaning of Memorial Day and peace.

8. Youngsters might even decorate war graves in local cemetery with tissue flowers made in Art. Spending a Saturday cleaning up cemetery area might be included.

9. Incorporate such words as *honor, parade, cemetery, peace* and *memory* into their spelling list for a week.

10. Letter to President stating their sentiments on wars in general. Penmanship and letter form and structure are essential here.

SUGGESTED LESSON GUIDES [1]

In this series of lessons the attempt is to create plans that can either tie together or, if need be, stand by themselves as workable, single units. That is, the lessons suggested can be used singly, in any multiple, or in any order. The lessons are behaviorally oriented and should involve as many students as possible.

It is beneficial that the teacher be informed as much as possible on the historical background and significance of Memorial Day before embarking on one of these lessons. Throughout the lessons themselves, and again in the bibliography, are suggested resources for locating this information. In any case, a quick, reliable, easily accessible source such as an encyclopedia would be adequate.

---

[1] Contributor: Mr. Andrew Case, Assistant Principal, Perkiomen Valley School, Pennsylvania.

Lesson Number One

Student Objectives

a) To recognize visual symbols associated with Memorial Day
b) To associate these symbols with their significance for Memorial Day
c) To conclude that Memorial Day is the common element in all visual symbols presented
d) To suggest and list additional visual symbols related to Memorial Day.

Materials Needed

a) Overhead projector
b) Five (5) transparencies of symbols
c) Several blank transparencies and grease pencil
d) Mimeographed scramble puzzle.

Procedure

This lesson is an introductory one in that it asks the student to examine a series of five pictures and identify the common factor concerning Memorial Day.

The teacher should project the pictures in this order:

1. Civil War battle picture
2. Gettysburg Address
3. Flowers
4. Flag at half mast
5. A tombstone or Arlington Cemetery.

Class members should be asked to identify each picture and suggest what the significance of each one is. Some *possible* responses might be:

Picture 1: a) obvious answer of Civil War battle scene
             b) war or fighting
             c) man's inability to get along
Picture 2: a) Abraham Lincoln (especially related with picture 1)

          b) Civil War (especially related with picture 1)

Picture 3: a) It is not unreasonable to assume that some students would begin to see total association at this point; answer of decorating dead soldiers' graves would be correct and appropriate here.

          b) flowers being symbol of peace

Picture 4: a) President Kennedy's assassination

          b) symbol of death in general (here, more students should begin to make connection and teacher should prompt this)

          c) hopefully, someone should see answer to be Memorial Day

Picture 5: a) again, death in general

          b) remembering those who have died (if no one in the class has identified Memorial Day to be the element of commonality, this answer should be expanded or even introduced by the teacher if need be).

          c) sadness (answers as general as these should be praised and expanded).

The class should be told before this that in addition to the recognition of the individual pictures, they are to look for associations among the five transparencies (each picture progressively identifies Memorial Day). It is easy to see that each picture has a connection when you know the overall answer. But in looking for the answer, other connections, just as sensible, can come to light. In our list of typical responses above, one can see that some of these specific identifications might also be valid as overall associations (e.g., Civil War, presidential assassination, death, war, etc.).

As soon as the discovery is made that all pictures relate to Memorial Day, the teacher should go back through the pictures, soliciting from the class what connection each one has, e.g., picture of Civil War battle—Memorial Day began following this war and has been broadened to include dead from all American wars; the picture of the flowers—original name of Decoration Day because of adorning the graves with flowers; the custom of flowers on the graves and cast onto water, honoring naval war dead (which is still widely used).

The concluding three pictures allow, and indeed call for, thorough coverage of the significance of Memorial Day and its solemnity. This idea should be stressed.

Summarizing Lesson One

Following thorough discussion, students should be asked to suggest, and even draw on blank transparencies, other possible associations. This activity, as with the next one, could very easily be given as an assignment with carryover to the next day.

Students can then act as the teacher in having their symbols explained by the class, e.g., students may draw or suggest a poppy, a parade, Lincoln Memorial, etc.

For homework, or again as an additional classroom activity, a mimeographed scramble puzzle utilizing ideas arrived at in this lesson can be introduced. This is included below as an option for the teacher.

Directions to Scramble Puzzle

From the clues given, complete blanks. Then unscramble the letters that are underlined twice. Your answer should be the whole idea of what we hope for each Memorial Day.

1) The original name for Memorial Day.
   __ __ __ __ __ __ __ __ __   __ __ __

2) Second word in name of the most famous speech associated with Memorial Day.
   __ __ __ __ __ __

3) New Symbol for Memorial Day.
   __ __ __ __ __

4) Date of this important holiday.
   __ __ __   __ __ __ __ __ __ __   __

5) First word to number 2.
   __ __ __ __ __ __ __ __
   __

Answers (for teacher)

1) Decoration Day
2) Address
3) Poppy
4) May Thirtieth
5) Gettysburg

Answer: PEACE

Resources for Lesson One

Several good summaries of Memorial Day for teacher and student information are:

George William Douglas, *The American Book of Days* (New York: H. W. Wilson Co., 1961), pp. 308–13.

Mary E. Hazeltine, *Anniversaries and Holidays* (Chicago: American Library Association, 1954), pp. 69, 89–90.

Elizabeth H. Sechrist, *Red Letter Days* (Philadelphia: Macrae Smith Co., 1965), pp. 124–30.

Memorial Day; Special Tribute, in U.S. History, and Now, Today (Kansas City: Americanism Department, V.F.W.).

Lesson Number Two

Student Objectives

a) To summarize the history and significance of Memorial Day
b) To analyze a popular folksong to discover both hidden and expressed meaning
c) To determine the relevance of this song to this holiday.

Materials Needed

a) Audio-visual equipment (filmstrip or motion picture projector, record player)
b) Recording, "Blowin' in the Wind"
c) (Optional)—Mimeographed scripts to song.

Procedure

The teacher can select, according to personal preference, grade level, and ability of the student, an appropriate audio-visual for presentation. This could give an overall, simple summary of the background of this holiday, its meaning, and its celebration, or it could be of a general nature leading to discussion. An example of this general type might be the movie, *How Sleep the Brave*, available through the Department of the Army.

If the securing of an audio-visual presents a problem, discussion of Memorial Day could begin from what the students know about the celebration of the holiday in their particular town or city. For example, elaboration on a theme of a float they may have seen in a local parade could easily bring out key facts regarding the significance of this holiday. For a very good summary of highlights and important basic information, the material in the free pamphlet, *Memorial Day; Special Tribute, in U.S. History, and Now, Today*, available through the V.F.W., is suggested.

From this quick summary, the class can be grouped to listen to a record of "Blowin' in the Wind." (Scripts can be distributed for students to follow.) Following this, each group is assigned to several tasks.

1) Analysis of meaning of key lines from the song (these could be underlined on each script)
2) Conclusion as to what the whole song is about
3) Conclusion as to the song's relevance to Memorial Day
4) Suggestions of other songs of same nature, e.g., "Where Have All the Flowers Gone?"

Summarizing Lesson Two

At the completion of the group work, each group should present its findings and share its reasoning with the others. (In all probability, findings and conclusions will not be identical, opening up the door for good, full group discussion.)

The song could be played again, following the interpretation given by the class, to create a different feeling for it by the students.

Lesson Two—"Blowin' in the Wind" [2]

(Song script could be purchased as needed.)

Lesson Number Three

A tremendous opportunity is provided in a study of Memorial Day for interdepartmental cooperation and organization. For this lesson, or lessons, depending on how deep you wish to go, the authors simply offer some suggestions for activities between departments or disciplines. This list, so to speak, is only the peel, with the full orange yet to be cut into.

In all probability, any study of Memorial Day would be undertaken by the social studies department, but cooperation is available and desirable between this and other areas.

Language Arts

a) Poem analysis and poem writing. Many famous poems have been written about Memorial Day by many famous poets. To name only a few: "Decoration Day," by Longfellow; "A Monument for the Soldiers," by James Whitcomb Riley; "A Ballad of Heroes," by Austin Dobson; "Cover Them Over With Beautiful Flowers," by Will Carleton; and "The Young Dead Soldiers," by Archibald MacLeish. Additional poems are suggested in *Granger's Index to Poetry* (Columbia University Press). Students could write their own poems with Memorial Day or any aspect of it as the central theme.

b) Short story reading and creative writing. Students could be given an opportunity to create a story about this holiday, perhaps its meaning today and in the past, perhaps a theme on the futility of war, or any other of a number of possibilities. Many short stories, either as examples or as activities in themselves, are available for the teacher. Again, to cite some examples: "The Drummer Boy of Shiloh," by Ray Bradbury; "For the Honor of the Com-

---

[2] Words and music by Bob Dylan.

pany," by Mary E. Mitchell; and "The Way to Glory," by Marian H. McNeeley. Many other short stories are suggested in the *Short Story Index* (H. W. Wilson Company).

Art

Here, investigation could be made of any art work associated with Memorial Day. Free drawing of each student's personal interpretation of Memorial Day is also an excellent activity. For interest and for publicity, the best pictures would be posted in school or published in the school and local newspaper.

Music

An examination of music associated with Memorial Day is worthwhile. An assembly could be organized featuring a school band and glee club to play and sing these songs that have been discovered by the students.

The avenues to explore are virtually endless, limited only by the teacher's and the students' imagination and cooperation. The approach in this suggested activity or activities is not the easy one to take. It is time consuming, thought provoking, and highly involved. But the end result, carefully striven for and followed through, will more than justify the effort expended.

Resources for Lesson Three

1. *The Complete Poetical Works of Longfellow* (Boston: Houghton Mifflin Co., Cambridge Edition), p. 359.
2. James Whitcomb Riley, "A Monument for the Soldiers," in *Poems for Red Letter Days,* ed. by Elizabeth H. Sechrist (Philadelphia: Macrae Smith Co.), p. 135.
3. *Ibid.,* p. 134.
4. Douglas, *The American Book of Days,* p. 311.
5. *Good Times Through Literature* (Chicago: Scott, Foresman and Co., 1957), p. 533.
6. *Adventures for Readers,* Book II (New York: Harcourt, Brace & World Inc., 1968), pp. 202–7.

7. Mary E. Mitchell, "For the Honor of the Company," in *Brother Against Brother*, ed. by Phyllis R. Fenner (New York: William Morrow Co., 1967), pp. 30–43.
8. Marian H. McNeeley, "The Way to Glory," in *Holiday Round-Up*, ed. by Lucille Pannell and Frances Cavanah (Philadelphia: Macrae Smith Co., 1950), pp. 184–94.

Lesson Number Four

Student Objectives

a) To hear and share both background information and personal meaning of Memorial Day
b) To associate information received into selection of pictorial symbols.
c) To express one's personal interpretation of Memorial Day.

Materials Needed

a) Procurement of materials and/or speaker from the American Legion or the Veterans of Foreign Wars (both associations are more than happy to help in matters of this nature).
b) Numerous pictorial magazines (*Life, Look, Newsweek,* etc.)

Procedure

The veterans' organizations are some of the best sources of material on the background history, significance, and current sentiment of Memorial Day. Arrangements for the sharing of these materials can be arranged through contact with any of the local branches of these groups.

Many children have little notion of the background and meaning of Memorial Day other than its being a day off from school; however, there are numerous ways to present the real meaning to them. Keeping in mind the other methods already suggested, one additional way could be through engaging an outside speaker.[3]

---

[3] There are arguments against using veterans' organizations for this purpose. Each community must be aware of public opinion in selecting an appropriate speaker.

The use of a guest speaker provides an advantage above other methods in that it allows the expression of another's personal feelings and firsthand information about war. We shall not belabor the use of a guest speaker, but we shall go into follow-up activities.

One activity found interesting and challenging is to have each pupil take a picture magazine and locate a picture, large or small, animate or inanimate, that, to the student, is relevant to the topic at hand. In this case, the picture must relate to something said by the speaker or to the subject of Memorial Day.

Each student is given a time limit to do this, and variations can be worked into it. For example, students can simply share pictures and explanations, or conduct a game in which the class tries to guess what meaning another student's picture relates to, or which student's picture is the most obvious or the most subtle.

Conclusion for Lesson Four

All in all, the lesson has done two broad things. It has helped students discover the meanings of Memorial Day through pictures most likely overlooked or given other meanings at other times, and it has exposed the class to a feeling for Memorial Day through the feelings of others.

Final Conclusion

All these suggested lessons or techniques are directed toward creating thought on the part of students about Memorial Day, not just as a name or another holiday. Each lesson is a bit different, yet all have basically the same goal in mind. As a holiday, Memorial Day has a special meaning all its own; it has no equal. This meaning can, and is, often overlooked. Perhaps we can develop in students the feeling that this is a day of great meaning and significance. And isn't that what it's all about???

BIBLIOGRAPHY AND SOURCE MATERIALS

Books

Adventures for Readers, Book II. New York: Harcourt, Brace & World, Inc., 1968.

The Complete Poetical Works of Longfellow. Cambridge edition. Boston: Houghton Mifflin Co.

Douglas, George W. *The American Book of Days.* New York: H. W. Wilson Co., 1961.

Fenner, Phyllis R., ed. *Brother Against Brother.* New York: William Morrow & Co., 1967.

Good Times Through Literature. Chicago: Scott, Foresman, and Co., 1957.

Granger's Index to Poetry. New York: Columbia University Press.

Hazeltine, Mary E. *Anniversaries and Holidays.* Chicago: American Library Association, 1954.

Pannell, Lucille, and Cavanah, Frances, eds. *Holiday Round-Up.* Philadelphia: Macrae Smith Co., 1950.

Sechrist, Elizabeth H., ed. *Poems for Red-Letter Days.* Philadelphia: Macrae Smith Co., 1951.

Sechrist, Elizabeth H., ed. *Red Letter Days.* Philadelphia: Macrae Smith Co., 1965.

Pamphlets

Americanism Department, V.F.W. *Memorial Day; Special Tributes in U.S. History, and Now, Today.* National Headquarters, Kansas City, Missouri.

Movies

Department of the Army, A.V. Support Center. *How Sleep the Brave.* Fort George B. Meade, Maryland.

5
Citizenship Day
September 17

Citizenship Day, especially in our present national mood, may well be one of our most effective days for emphasizing responsibilities, obligations and individual rights. It is possible for every teacher to do much to establish the seeds that may blossom into the proper active attitude, which we all hope to encourage in all of our classes. Building responsible citizenship is one of the primary aims of public education. We are sure that, given the proper creative setting, youngsters of all ages would be deeply interested in seeing their best work recognized and experiencing a spirit of pride for a job well done.

PERTINENT FACTS

1. The Declaration of Independence by the Representatives of the United States of America in Congress assembled, July 4, 1776, ". . . dissolved the political bands which have connected them. . . ."
2. Pledge of Allegiance: "I pledge allegiance to the flag of the United States of America and to the republic for which it stands, one nation, under God, indivisible, with liberty and justice for all."
3. James Madison of Virginia, who became the fourth president of the United States, is known as "the father of the Constitution." He kept a complete journal of all that went on at the Constitu-

tional Convention in 1787. This was published after his death as the *Journal of the Federal Convention*. Because of this journal, we know much of what the delegates thought as they composed the Constitution. One of Madison's ideas, the separation of powers, became an important principle of the Constitution. After the document was finished it was presented to the thirteen states for ratification. Madison played an important role in helping to get the Constitution ratified (approved) by the states. He joined with Alexander Hamilton and John Jay in writing a number of essays in favor of ratification. These essays were called *The Federalist*.

4. You may be a citizen if (Amendment XIV, July 28, 1868, Section I):

    "All persons born or naturalized in the United States . . ."

5. The States of the United States of America—Dates of Admission—Capitols.

6. Presidents of the United States—States of Origin—Terms of Office—Parties they represented.

7. How does the Bill of Rights protect each one of us today?
    (1) You have little fear that there will be a knock on the door some dark night and a storm trooper will demand that you accompany him to the nearest station house because you took part in an orderly demonstration against government policy. Why not? Let's look at the first amendment to the Constitution of the United States. What rights does it protect for each of us?

Amendment #1

"Congress shall make no law respecting an establishment of religion, or prohibiting the free exercise thereof; or abridging the freedom of speech, or of the press; or the right of the people peaceably to assemble, and to petition the Goverment for a redress of grievances."

(2) Recently, a passenger aboard a Pacific Airlines plane shot the pilot and co-pilot. The plane crashed, killing all forty-four persons aboard. A few weeks later a sixteen-year-old boy fired

nine shots from two pistols into the floor of a DC-8 flying from Melbourne, Florida, to New Orleans. You will find that "the right of the people to keep and bear arms" has been limited by decisions of the Supreme Court. Licensing of pistols and other firearms has been found necessary in order to prevent such incidents as those described in this paragraph.

Amendment #2

"A well-regulated militia being necessary to the security of a free state, the right of the people to keep and bear arms shall not be infringed."

(3) "Due to the Vietnam situation I am assigning six soldiers to your house," explained the Captain. "You are to feed them, clothe them and provide them with fine beds to sleep in."
"But I have no room and my husband cannot afford to provide soldiers with food and clothing," pleaded the poor housewife.
"Too bad! Do it or else."
During colonial times this was frequently done. What amendment to the Constitution protects us against such an outrageous situation here in the United States of America?

Amendment #3

"No soldier shall, in time of peace, be quartered in any house, without the consent of the owner; nor in time of war, but in a manner to be prescribed by law."

(4) Recently, a prominent sports figure was stopped and arrested for speeding. During the arresting procedures the individual claimed that he was pushed around, searched for no apparent reason, and abused by the arresting officers. Does the fourth amendment provide protection against such practices?

Amendment #4

"The right of the people to be secure in their persons, houses, papers, and effects, against unreasonable searches and seizures, shall not be violated; and no warrants shall issue but upon probable cause, supported by oath or affirmation, and particularly describing the place to be searched, and the persons or things to be seized."

(5) During a grand jury hearing a subpoenaed witness was asked if he claimed ownership to the one million dollars found in his abandoned garage. He answered by "taking the fifth." What does this amendment do for the individual? Why would he refuse to answer?

Amendment #5

"No person shall be held to answer for a capital, or otherwise infamous crime, unless on a presentment or indictment of a grand jury, except in cases arising in the land or naval forces, or in the militia, when in actual service in time of war or public danger; nor shall any person be subject for the same offense to be twice put in jeopardy of life or limb; nor shall be compelled, in any criminal case, to be a witness against himself; nor be deprived of life, liberty, or property, without due process of law; nor shall private property be taken for public use, without just compensation."

(6) Two young thugs in search of money and thrills molested, robbed and beat a seventy-five-year-old man on the subway. Two youths were later arrested by the police on an anonymous tip in the form of a typewritten letter. The anonymous writer feared to come forward and be a witness against the accused. Does the evidence hold up in court? Suppose the old-aged victim finds it difficult to tell definitely who beat him. What does the sixth amendment say?

Amendment #6

"In all criminal prosecutions, the accused shall enjoy the right to a speedy and public trial, by an impartial jury of the state and district wherein the crime shall have been committed, which district shall have been previously ascertained by law, and to be informed of the nature and cause of the accusation; to be confronted with the witnesses against him; to have compulsory process for obtaining witnesses in his favor, and to have the assistance of counsel for his defense."

(7) Despite repeated requests for the landlord to repair the main steps to your tenement apartment, the steps remain loose, broken and rotted. During the afternoon your youngest son, four years old, falls through the steps, breaking an arm and hip socket. Do you have the legal right to a jury trial when you sue the landlord? What amendment to the Constitution provides you with this right?

Amendment #7

"In suits at common law, where the value in controversy shall exceed twenty dollars, the right of trial by jury shall be preserved, and no fact tried by a jury shall be otherwise re-examined in any court of the United States than according to the rules of the common law."

(8) Several senators are championing a bill to do away with high bail and in some cases with bail itself. They claim that it is unfair, particularly to the poor. What amendment deals with bail, fines, and punishment?

Amendment #8

"Excessive bail shall not be required, nor excessive fines imposed, nor cruel and unusual punishment inflicted."

(9) Is it possible to list all the rights of the people? Are any provisions made by the authors of the Constitution to guarantee those rights not listed in the Constitution? Let's look at the ninth amendment.

Amendment #9

"The enumeration in the Constitution, of certain rights, shall not be construed to deny or disparage others retained by the people."

(10) Many of the southern states, as well as some northern states, refer to the Constitution when arguing such issues as integration, civil rights, and establishment of certain state laws. What amendment do they most frequently refer to?

Amendment #10

"The powers not delegated to the United States by the Constitution, nor prohibited by it to the states, are reserved to the states respectively, or to the people."

A number of delegates to the Constitutional Convention of 1787 were dissatisfied with the document when it was finished. One of these was George Mason of Virginia. A friend and neighbor of George Washington, he had been a member of the Virginia Convention of 1776. This body drew up the first written constitution of any state in America. It contained a Declaration of Rights, which Mason drafted. When our original Constitution was issued without a Bill of Rights, Mason refused to sign even though he had been one of the authors. In Virginia he argued against ratification of the Constitution. His arguments were so powerful that the first Congress drew up ten amendments, which constitute the Bill of Rights. These were ratified and became part of our Constitution in 1791, shortly before George Mason died. Thus, he lived to see the Constitution improved as a result of his efforts.

8. What additional rights are guaranteed in the other amendments?
   (1) It is difficult to amend the Constitution. Article V of the Constitution tells how this may be done. Most amendments have been proposed by two-thirds of each House (Senate and House of Representatives) of Congress. They have been ratified (approved) by the legislature of three-quarters of the states. Since we now have fifty states, an amendment must be approved by thirty-eight states before it can become part of our Constitution.
   (2) The Bill of Rights (first ten amendments) became part of our Constitution, as we have learned, in 1791. Since that time only fourteen amendments have been adopted. Let us see how several of these have improved our democratic government.

(3) The thirteenth amendment abolished slavery. It provided, "Neither slavery nor involuntary servitude except as a punishment for crime whereof the party shall have been duly convicted, shall exist within the United States, or any place subject to their jurisdiction."

(4) The fourteenth amendment is an extension of the Bill of Rights protecting the people against unjust state laws. It starts by indicating who are citizens. It provides:

"All persons born or naturalized in the United States, and subject to the jurisdiction thereof, are citizens of the United States and of the state wherein they reside."

(5) The fourteenth amendment goes on to tell what rights the states may not take away. It says:

"No state shall make or enforce any law which shall abridge the privileges or immunities of citizens of the United States, nor shall any state deprive any person of life, liberty or property without due process of law, nor deny to any person within its jurisdiction the equal protection of the laws."

This part of the Constitution, reinforced by laws recently passed by Congress, is at last being put into full effect. It will insure equal civil rights and opportunities, education, voting, employment, travel and residence to all Americans.

(6) The fifteenth amendment, adopted after the Civil War, attempted to guarantee the right to vote to the former slaves. It stated:

"The right of the citizens of the United States to vote shall not be denied or abridged by the United States on account of race, color, or previous condition of servitude."

Several of the states got around this provision by requiring voters to pay a tax (poll tax) as a privilege for voting. This was outlawed by the twenty-fourth amendment, adopted in 1964. It provides:

"The right of citizens of the United States to vote in any primary or other election for President or Vice-President or for electors for President or Vice-President, or for Senator or Representative in Congress, shall not be denied or abridged by the United States or any state by reason of failure to pay any poll tax or other tax."

(7) Another important amendment, the nineteenth, extended the right to vote to women. It was adopted in 1920 after women had taken an active part in helping to win World War I. It provides:

"The right of citizens of the United States to vote shall not be denied or abridged by the United States or by any state on account of sex."

(8) The twenty-third amendment, adopted in 1961, granted to citizens of the District of Columbia (Washington, D.C.) the right to vote for President and Vice-President. Citizens who live in our capitol city still do not vote for U.S. Senators or Congressmen, and they do not take part in the government of their own city. Some day soon it is hoped these rights will also be granted to them.

(9) Under the original Constitution all United States Senators were elected by their state legislatures. The people had no say in choosing members of the United States Senate. This was changed by the seventeenth amendment in 1913. It says:

"The Senate of the United States shall be composed of two Senators from each state, elected by the people thereof, for six years and each Senator shall have one vote."

(10) Article VI of the original Constitution contains a provision worth noting as we study the various guarantees under our supreme law. In clause #3 of this article it is provided that ". . . no religious test shall ever be required as a qualification to any office or public trust under the United States."

SUGGESTED CLASSROOM ACTIVITIES

1. Write your representatives in government, expressing your individual views concerning some vital issue. State your interest, be brief, express your desire, thank him for his consideration, be sure your letter is properly written, give your name and address.
2. How do you address your public official?
   In Washington
   In state capital
   In your town
3. Report on:
   Qualifications for voting and registering
   When, where and how to vote
   The absentee ballot
   How to enroll in a political party
   Nominations and the primary
   General elections.
4. How does a state serve its citizens?
5. What does a citizen owe his state?
6. List questions to ask political leaders.
7. How do you analyze political structure?
8. What did these famous leaders mean?

Thomas Jefferson:

"I have sworn upon the altar of God, eternal hostility against every form of tyranny over the mind of man."

Benjamin Franklin:

"They that give up essential liberty to obtain a little temporary safety, deserve neither liberty nor safety."

Erasmus:

"They may chain the tongues of men; they cannot touch their minds."

9. The teacher might wish to develop a sociometric diagram of the class.
10. Develop role-playing and socio-dramas as a technique for discovering how people feel about a given situation.
11. Survey community services and opportunities.
    a. Recreation
    b. Employment
    c. Health
    d. Library
    e. Zoning, etc.
12. Make up cartoons for political reaction.
13. Display bulletin board materials.
14. Do creative editorial writing.
15. Have "password" games.
16. Play "To Tell the Truth."
17. Skits.
18. Panels.
19. Debates.
20. What are the means of acquiring knowledge about community problems?
21. Discussion of civil rights and liberties.
22. Write a composition to be published in the school paper and local newspaper: "School Citizenship and Mutual Respect."
23. Select many excerpts from the citizenship compositions for a local newspaper; have photographer take pictures, and make a centrally located bulletin board display.
24. Publish one or two compositions in the local paper each night for an appropriate period of time.
25. Have many youngsters sign up to visit with senior citizen groups.
26. Have youngsters recite some interesting piece such as Red Skelton's "Pledge of Allegiance," as recited by Red Skelton in terms of his childhood.

SUGGESTED LESSON GUIDES

Lesson Number One

Understanding the Preamble to the Constitution of the United States may well be the spark to realizing what we have as citizens of the United States of America and what it really means for all of us.

First, let's read the Preamble. I will read it orally and you follow reading it silently to yourself. Keep in mind: What national goals does the Preamble announce?

> "We, the people of the United States, in order to form a more perfect union, establish justice and insure domestic tranquillity, provide for the common defense, promote the general welfare, and secure the blessings of liberty to ourselves and our posterity, do ordain and establish this Constitution for the United States of America."

These are beautiful words and are loaded with meaning for each of us. In the next four days we are going to analyze the Preamble and try to understand what we have read.

Lesson Number Two

The first thing we read as we open the Constitution of the United States is the Preamble. The authors of the Constitution started right in by stating their goals just as you would if you were starting a club. Let's take the Preamble apart, word for word, to understand its vast meaning. This will help us understand the rest of the Constitution as we study it.

WE, THE PEOPLE OF THE UNITED STATES, . . .

Does this mean all the people or only those who were writing the Constitution? Does it mean those who were not citizens? You will find that the Constitution protects us all equally. Discussion and debates may follow.

IN ORDER TO FORM A MORE PERFECT UNION, . . .

Remember, the thirteen colonies declared themselves free from England by adopting the Declaration of Independence on July 4, 1776. As you know, this document set in writing the belief that "all men are created equal" and have a right to "life, liberty, and the pursuit of happiness." For these beliefs many good men fought and died until the independence of the United States of America was recognized by England at the Treaty of Paris in 1783. However, victory did not bring a new, strong government into being. In fact, as you will recall, since 1781 the states were loosely united under an agreement called the Articles of Confederation. This "league of friendship" established a very weak government because each state looked out for itself without regard to the welfare of all. It was therefore necessary "to form a more perfect union" if the new nation was to survive.

ESTABLISH JUSTICE, . . .

The Constitution of the new nation must see to it that every man, woman and child is protected. In addition, every person must be given the privileges for which the War for Independence was fought. The new government must be based on law. Equality before the law must be carefully protected. In other words, the Constitution must "establish justice."

INSURE DOMESTIC TRANQUILLITY, . . .

Look up the word *tranquillity*. Why is it important to "insure domestic tranquillity"? Can a country prosper if this is not done? How is domestic tranquillity brought about without interfering with justice? This is one of the things our Constitution tries to do.

PROVIDE FOR THE COMMON DEFENSE, . . .

You will recall that the new country was surrounded by territory held by powerful Europeans. Spain, France and England held territory in North America. The new nation, just as today, had to make plans for its defense. This was one of the goals written into the Preamble.

PROMOTE THE GENERAL WELFARE, . . .

There were many ways for the nation to help its people. The departments of the treasury and of the post office were just two of them. Roads and canals had to be built. Courts had to be established. Patents and copyrights would protect inventors and authors. Sound money had to be issued to help business. These are just some of the ways for the new nation to "promote the general welfare."

AND SECURE THE BLESSINGS OF LIBERTY TO OURSELVES AND OUR POSTERITY, . . .

The Constitution would help keep us free as long as we lived under it. It would continue to keep us free from generation to generation.

DO ORDAIN AND ESTABLISH THIS CONSTITUTION FOR THE UNITED STATES OF AMERICA.

The goals that the writing of the Constitution hoped to accomplish are stated in the Preamble. The last phrase tells us that the Constitution is the plan of government for the United States of America. It was written and adopted in order to secure the lofty goals set forth in the Preamble.

Lessons Numbers Three and Four

Understanding What You Have Read

1. Which of these facts can you find in the previous discussion?
    a) The reason why the Constitution was written
    b) The powers of the President and Vice-President
    c) Why it was necessary "to provide for the common defense"
    d) How the states were governed before the Constitution was adopted.

2. Which of these questions may be answered as a result of your studies?
   a) What is a preamble?
   b) What is the meaning of the phrase, "to form a more perfect union"?
   c) What are the duties of the United States Supreme Court?
   d) Why was the United States Constitution established?
3. What is the main idea of this discussion?
   a) To describe the problems of the new nation
   b) To tell why the Constitution was written
   c) To review the War for Independence
   d) To show the courage of the founding fathers.
4. *Knowing why,* choose the item or items that best complete the statement.
   a) The Constitution had to "provide for the common defense" because:
      (1) the United States was a wilderness
      (2) we were without a militia or an army
      (3) we were menaced by hostile foreign powers—England, France, Spain
      (4) there were dangerous Indian tribes on our borders
      (5) we were a new nation.
   b) It was necessary "to form a more perfect union" because:
      (1) there were serious disagreements among the states
      (2) there was no Union when the Constitution was written
      (3) the war with England was still going on
      (4) the Articles of Confederation were not satisfactory
      (5) the government was weak.
   c) The phrase, "to promote the general welfare" included:
      (1) aid to business and industry
      (2) building of roads and canals
      (3) guaranteed jobs for all
      (4) free public education
      (5) patents and copyrights.
   d) It was necessary "to insure domestic tranquillity" because:
      (1) the War for Independence was over
      (2) the states were weak

(3) law and order was not firmly established

(4) prosperity depended on good government

(5) the soldiers had returned home.

e) The phrase "to establish justice" included:

(1) equality before the law

(2) jobs for all

(3) pensions for soldiers

(4) guarantees of legal protection for anyone accused of crime

(5) equal rights for men and women.

Lessons Five and Six

True or False

Reread the Preamble and its discussion and find the sentences in the text that prove whether each of the following statements is true or false.

1. The Constitution gives protection only to United States citizens.

2. The independence of the United States was recognized by the Treaty of Paris in 1783.

3. The Constitution established a "league of friendship."

4. When the Constitution was written, the United States was surrounded by territory held by powerful European nations.

5. The authors of the Constitution had in mind future generations when they wrote the Preamble.

Developing Ideas and Skills

The Preamble states six reasons for establishing the Constitution of the United States. List the six reasons *in the order of their importance,* placing the most important reason first and so forth. Give arguments to prove your judgment is right.

Summing Up

Fill in the box at the right with your own explanation of the meaning of the phrases of the Preamble.

PREAMBLE PHRASE	MEANING
1. To form a more perfect union	
2. To establish justice	
3. To insure domestic tranquillity	
4. To provide for the common defense	
5. To promote the general welfare	
6. To insure the blessings to ourselves and our posterity	

BIBLIOGRAPHY AND SOURCE MATERIALS

Challenge to Americans. The struggle we face and how to help with it. Advertising Council, 25 W. 45th Street, New York, N.Y.

Connecticut. William Buckley and Charles Perry. Oxford Book Co., 1953.

Connecticut Voters Manual. 1969. Secretary of State, State Capitol, Hartford, Conn.

League of Women Voters of Connecticut. 44 Farmington Avenue, Hartford, Conn.

News and Views. Connecticut Public Expenditure Council, 21 Lewis Street, Hartford, Conn. (Views concerning current political issues.)

State of Connecticut Register and Manual. Annually. Hartford, Conn.

Techniques Useful in Citizenship Education. Connecticut State Department of Education, Hartford, Conn.

The Task of Citizenship Education. Bulletin 50. Connecticut State Department of Education, Hartford, Conn.

General Readings

American Council for Nationalities Service. *How to Become a Citizen of the United States.* 20th ed. Oceana, 1963.

Appleby, Paul H. *Citizens as Sovereigns.* Syracuse, N.Y.: Syracuse University Press, 1962.

Bard, Harry, and others. *Citizenship and Government in Modern America.* New York: Holt, Rinehart and Winston, 1966.

Barth, Alan. *Heritage of Liberty.* New York: McGraw-Hill, Inc., 1965.

Brooks, Alexander D. *A Bibliography of Civil Rights and Civil Liberties.* Civil Liberties Education Foundation, 1962.

Citizenship Education. Bureau of Secondary Curriculum Development. New York State Department, Albany, N.Y.

Hughes, Ray O. *Today's Problems: Social, Political, Economic Issues Facing America.* Rev. Ed. Boston: Allyn and Bacon, 1962.

Johnson, Gerald W. *This American People.* New York: Harper & Row, 1951. (The rights and duties of citizenship in the United States described historically.)

Life International. *Nine Who Chose America.* New York: E. P. Dutton & Co., 1959.

Making Better Citizens. Civil Education Foundation, 5 Chauncey Street, Cambridge, Mass.

Practical Political Action. Tufts University, Medford, Mass. 1962. (A guide for young citizens.)

Richards, W. Marvin, and Isely, B. *We the People.* 2nd ed. Chicago: Beckley-Cardy Co., 1964.

Rienow, Robert. *The Citizen and His Government: Rights and Responsibilities.* Houghton, 1963.

Scholastic Magazines. *What You Should Know About Democracy, and Why.* Four Winds, 1965.

School Civic Clubs. Board of Education, New York, N.Y. (A teacher's guide.)

Starratt, Edith E., *et al. Our American Government Today.* Englewood Cliffs, N.J.: Prentice-Hall, 1958.

United States Immigration and Naturalization Service, Justice Department. *Gateway to Citizenship.* Rev. ed. Washington, D.C.: U.S. Government Printing Office, 1962.

Wagner, Ruth H., and Green, I. E. *Put Democracy to Work.* Rev. ed. Abelard-Schuman, 1961. (Traces citizenship from ancient Greece to the present.)

Weaver, Warren. *Making Our Government Work: The Challenge of American Citizenship.* Coward-McCann, 1964.

What You Should Know About Democracy and Why. Scholastic Magazine, New York, N.Y., 1964. (Adapted from a series of articles published under the same title in *World Week* and *Senior Scholastic.*)

6
Thanksgiving Day
Using the Newspaper

Thanksgiving, as every school youngster knows, is a time for giving thanks, a time for counting one's blessings, and a time for warm friendship as originally represented between the early New England settlers and the Indians. However, to keep the theme timely and meaningful, one must recognize that Thanksgiving celebrations are also marked by controversy. A number of popular posters prior to the holiday have proclaimed the following:

"THANKSGIVING? FOR VIETNAM? ATTICA? LAOS? PAKISTAN? CAIRO?"

The text accompanying such posters would read as follows:

"Joining with Vietnam Veterans against the war in a dawn to dusk fast at the State Capitol on Thanksgiving Day, Thursday, November 25, we will fast, then conduct a memorial service for the victims of the war in Indochina at dusk. All are invited to participate at any time during that period. Vets all over the country will be having similar services and the G.I.'s in Vietnam will join the Quakers at Quang Ngai in a service in Vietnam in addition to boycotting their turkey dinner. We cannot indulge ourselves with a sumptuous meal while so many suffer at our Nation's hands in Vietnam. We seek all who participate to make a contribution for those Vietnamese civilians who have lost limbs in this conflict. . . ."

Such activities by outspoken groups suggest some challenging instructional opportunities for the classroom teacher. There is an increasing need for more balanced activities for youngsters as they participate in Thanksgiving programs and study.

PERTINENT FACTS

1. 1972 marks the 351st anniversary of the traditional feast day that began at Plymouth, Massachusetts in 1621.
2. The essence of the first celebration was an offering of thanks to the Almighty for surviving the first year in the wilderness.
3. Attending the first Thanksgiving Day with the Pilgrims were about ninety Wampanoag Indians who had helped the Pilgrims survive.
4. Thanksgiving Day did *not* catch on and become a national custom. It was quite the opposite. Thanksgiving as a holiday disappeared from American life shortly after the Pilgrims had that legendary turkey feast and might never have reappeared had it not been for a little-known New Jersey congressman named Elias Boudinot.
5. Representative Boudinot was a deeply religious man who was a founder and first president of the American Bible Society. In 1789, the annals of the House of Representatives of the Congress of the United States reported:

> He [Representative Boudinot] could not think of letting the session pass over without offering an opportunity to all the citizens of the United States for joining, with one voice, in returning to Almighty God their sincere thanks for the many blessings He has poured down upon them.

   Boudinot introduced a resolution requesting the President to set aside a day of public thanksgiving and prayer.
6. Representative Roger Sherman of Connecticut leaped to Boudinot's support with copious biblical quotations suggesting that the proposal was warranted by a number of precedents in holy writ. He cited, for example, the solemn thanksgiving and

rejoicing that took place in the time of Solomon after the building of the temple.

7. President George Washington issued a proclamation in 1789 setting aside the last Thursday in November as a national day of thanksgiving ". . . for the many signal favors of Almighty God especially by affording the people of America an opportunity peaceably to establish a constitution of government for their safety and happiness."

8. That first Thanksgiving dinner was a "men only" affair. There were no Indian squaws, and for all practical purposes the Pilgrim women did all the kitchen chores and did not actually participate in the festival.

9. The first Thanksgiving Day lasted for three days, and the Indians outnumbered their hosts by about two to one.

10. "The First Thanksgiving Proclamation":

The New York Public Library's Manuscript Division has turned up this historical rediscovery: the first Thanksgiving proclamation. This document ordaining a day of thanks and prayer in the Berkeley settlement in Virginia was issued in 1619 —before Governor Bradford established the famous celebration in 1623 for the Plymouth Colony in Massachusetts.

* * *

Ordinances direcçons and Instructions to Captaine John Woodleefe for the gouerment of men and servante in the Towne and hundered of [Berkeley] in Virginia giuen by [Sir William Throckmorton], knight and barronet Richard [Berkeley] esq., George Thorpe esq., and John Smyth, gent, wherevnto our comission of the date hereof made to the said captaine Woodleefe hath reference.

1. Impr wee ordaine that the day of our ships arrivall at the place assigned for plantaçon in the land of Virginia shall be yearly and perputualy kept holy as a day of thanksgiuing to Almight god.

2. I wee doe ordaine that the lorde day be keept in holy and religious order and that all bodily labour and vaine sporte and scandolous recreations be refrained, and that

morning and evening prayer (according to the english booke of common prayer) be Dayly read and attended vnto and such other divine exercisses of preaching and reading to be on the same day used, as it shall please god to enable the minister for the tyme there being to pforme.

3. I wee doe ordayne and direct, that you our gouernor and all our people and servants assemble togeather once a day to prayer, imediately after yhe forenoone labour ended and before dinner. . . .

5. I wee doe ordayne and direct that imediately after the place of habitaçon is agreed vppon in manner aforesaid, that [you] cause [forthwith] to be erected houses fit for the present shelter and succor of our people [which] as wee suppose, may be for the better expediçon built homelike and to be couered [with] bordes; of [which] we commend to [your] especiall care the framing of twoo, where of the one for the safe keeping of the tooles implemente of husbandry powder, shott, Armor, and victuall, [which] wee wish may be be strongly planted on the inside: And the other for your assemblies at time of prayer and time of diet. . . .

* * *

[Indorsed:] Copy of Instructions geven to Captayne Woodleefe. 4 Sept. 1619.[1]

UTILIZATION OF THE NEWSPAPER IN THE CLASSROOM

The newspaper can play a significant part in stimulating the instructional program in the classroom. Why use the newspaper in the classroom? Consider the following:

1. The newspaper is an up-to-date supplement of the materials in the textbook and is easily available.
2. The newspaper contains special holiday items, which can be used in any subject area and can also show the correlation between subjects.

---

[1] "The First Thanksgiving Proclamation," *The New York Times,* Thursday, November 25, 1971.

3. The newspaper can be used with any group in school regardless of age or ability level.
4. The use of the newspaper is limited only by the limits of the ingenuity of the teacher.
5. The newspaper is inexpensive.
6. The newspaper allows each student to have fresh materials in his hands each day.
7. The newspaper brings fresh holiday materials directly to the student on each occasion.
8. The newspaper can be adapted to the needs of any learning activity.

LESSON PLAN GUIDELINES

Lesson Number One

Tell the story of Thanksgiving by reading, or by interpreting pictures from the newspapers and magazines. Given a picture of youngsters at a street settlement house who are enjoying a Thanksgiving dinner, the teacher might deal with such questions as:

1. What does this picture mean to you?
2. Do you know what a street settlement house is?
3. Do we have any organizations in our own community that might be comparable to a settlement house?
4. Write whatever thoughts come into your head as you view this picture.
5. What about the expressions on the faces of the youngsters—do they tell you something?
6. What do you think the young adult in the picture is doing there?

There are numerous pictures printed in newspapers during the Thanksgiving Season depicting family Thanksgiving dinners now and in the past. These may be in the form of photographs or paintings such as those by Norman Rockwell. The questions offered below are the kind that can generate many creative endeavors by pupils:

1. What does this picture say to you?
2. Name the items on the table.
3. Who is Norman Rockwell?
4. Have you seen any other paintings by Norman Rockwell?
5. Can you guess the period of time this picture might represent?
6. Does this period of time mean anything to your parents?
7. Tell a humorous story about this picture.
8. Tell a mysterious story about this picture.
9. Is there a message in this picture?
10. Make up a caption for this picture.
11. Tell a sad story about this picture.
12. Tell a happy story about this picture.

Lesson Number Two

Select an article or an editorial in your local newspaper dealing with the Thanksgiving theme. This can provide the basis for a vocabulary exercise, and you can use it for developing dictionary skills as well. Using the article, consider the following learning activities:

1. Suggestions for classroom assignments:
    a. Find Plymouth and Cape Cod on the map.
    b. What state are they in?
2. Select ten spelling words from this article. Write the dictionary meaning and pronunciation. These will be your personal vocabulary enrichment words. Use them in a sentence.
3. Interpret selected passages and elaborate on various thoughts in the article:
    a. What are the main ideas in these editorials or articles?
    b. Can you draw some inferences from them? Name the passage and your inference.
4. Divide the class into small interest groups and assign appropriate tasks.

Lesson Number Three

Letters to the Editor:

In most newspapers there usually is a column of this nature. In this area of the paper many people pour out their hearts and souls.

Frequently, a human interest story appears that can stimulate discussion and other activities. The questions below would be helpful in dealing with such topics:

1. The message in this story is thought-provoking and heart-warming. What do you think of as you read it?
2. What is a human interest story? Is it the type of story that deals with amusing, unusual, or emotional topics that are a reflection of some major issue? Discuss this in class. What do your friends and parents say is the definition of a human interest story?

Lesson Number Four

Research and Critical Analysis:

Select an article that may be stimulating or even controversial and guide the pupils through a study, research and analysis of it. Consider these guidelines:

1. For many able students the article could be the springboard for future study.
2. It may be used to explain the place of the historian in our society.
3. It may provide the vehicle for contemporary issues such as the Black Man's place in American society, the draft, the war, the economy, and religious oppression in Ireland.
4. The possibilities for vocabulary and spelling exercises in an article are almost endless. Homonyms, pronunciation, definitions, dividing into syllables, keys for vowels, roots, details, comprehension, drawing inferences, and critical thinking are also encompassed.

5. Research into the background of the author may provide information that could give some insights into why and how the article was written.

SUGGESTED CLASSROOM ACTIVITIES

1. Draw a series of typical Thanksgiving Day scenes and write an original caption.
2. Develop a bulletin board with newspaper clippings on the Thanksgiving theme.
3. Make a typical sand table or model of an early Pilgrim settlement.
4. Write original news releases, as if you were there in 1621.
5. Do a series on the customs of the times.
6. Do a series on the backgrounds of the early settlers at Plymouth.
7. Give a slide presentation of the first year at Plymouth.
8. Write an original skit or play on the life of the early settlers.
9. Develop a comedy or "spoof" about the early colonial days.
10. Develop a comedy on the part the Indians might have played at Plymouth.

Suggested Five-day Lesson Plan:

This unit is intended to help students reach an understanding and appreciation of the heritage of our colonial forefathers. The importance of individual and group effort will be highlighted as the basic reason for the survival of colonial Americans.

Moreover, it is designed to help students carry the attitude of cooperation into their interpersonal relationships as members of families, groups, and societies.

Some Appropriate Objectives:

1. To help the students appreciate the Pilgrims as people.
2. To understand the quest for religious freedom.
3. To learn about the colonial ways of living.
4. To understand the major values of yesterday.

5. To appreciate the early ways of creativity as essential for survival of the period.
6. To understand the problems of a people in a new country.
7. To study about some great people.
8. To learn how to gather information, analyze material, and effectively develop projects.
9. To organize correctly facts and materials.
10. To develop a familiarity with information and terms in the history lesson.
11. To develop the ability to interpret one's readings and observations.
12. To develop skill in recording observations and findings.
13. To list reasons for the Pilgrims' coming to America.
14. To develop skills for working with people. Pupils should be able to:

    a. Participate in discussion
    b. Display cooperation when in group activities
    c. Practice helping others
    d. Adhere to rules of politeness such as taking turns in discussions
    e. Share ideas of other people
    f. Recognize that each person's services contribute to the general outcome of a task.

Activities:

1. View an exhibit of maps, pictures and objects of the Pilgrims and the Mayflower.
2. View a film, such as "Pilgrims"—16mm, 22 minutes—their persecution, life in Holland, crossing to New England, first year here.
3. Discuss events leading to the Pilgrimage.
4. View a filmstrip, such as "New England—Motivation Behind Colonizing."
5. Costume designing.
6. Early crafts show.

7. Original cooking sampling.
8. Sing folk songs of period.
9. Have a play.
10. Have a Thanksgiving feast.

Suggested Culminating Activities:

1. Prepare a Thanksgiving feast:
    a. Costumes
    b. Food
    c. Crafts
2. Have a discussion of some of the problems of the unit just completed.
3. Have individual groups present their efforts to the class.
4. Visit Plymouth Plantation if you're in the Boston, Mass. area.
5. Make collection of pictures on phases of Pilgrim life and use them in opaque projector, having students comment on them.
6. Make a series of displays.

Suggested Means of Evaluation:

1. Class should discuss aims of unit and try to determine which ones were met best and least.
2. Observation by teacher of growth of attitudes and skills.
3. Observation of committee work by teacher.
4. Comments of students on their own growth, or skills they have acquired.

BIBLIOGRAPHY AND RESOURCE MATERIALS

Books for Teachers:

Bradford, William. *Of Plymouth Plantation, 1620–1647.* New ed. New York: Alfred Knopf, 1952.

Dorset, Phyllis Flanders. *Historic Ships Afloat.* New York: Macmillan Co., 1957.

James, Sydney V. *Three Visitors to Early Plymouth.* Available document at Plymouth Plantation.

Langdon, George D., Jr. *Pilgrim Colony.* New Haven: Yale University Press, 1966.

Luckhardt, Mildred Corell. *Thanksgiving—Feast and Festival.* Available at Plymouth Plantation.

McIntyre, Ruth A. *Debts Hopeful and Desparate.* Economic insight into the venture. Available at Plymouth Plantation.

Morison, Samuel Eliot. *The Story of the "Old Colony" of New Plymouth 1620–1692.* New York: Alfred Knopf, 1956.

Morison, Samuel Eliot. *The Oxford History of the American People.* New York: Oxford University Press, 1965.

Powers, Edwin. *Crime and Punishment in Early Massachusetts, 1620–1692.* Documentary history available at Plymouth Plantation.

Time-Life Books. *Age of Exploration.* New York: Time Inc., 1966.

Others Books:

Adams, James Truslow. *Album of Colonial History.* New York: Charles Scribner's Sons, 1944.

American Heritage, editors. *The American Heritage Cookbook and Illustrated History of American Eating and Drinking.* New York: American Heritage Publishing Co., Inc., 1964.

Andrews, Charles McLean. *The Colonial Period of American History.* New Haven: Yale University Press, 1936.

Beeton, Isabella. *Book of Household Management.* London: S. O. Beeton and Co., 1861.

Bennett, H., ed. *The Chemical Formulary.* Vol. III. New York: Chem. Publishing Co., Inc.

Boorstin, David J. *The Americans: The Colonial Experience.* New York: Random House, 1958.

Bradley, Carolyn C. *Western World Costume*. New York: D. Appleton, 1954.

Cable, Mary. *American Manners and Morals*. New York: American Heritage Publishing Co., 1969.

Chalmers, Helena. *Clothes On and Off the Stage—A History of Dress From the Earliest Times to the Present*. New York: D. Appleton, 1928.

Cunnington, Phillis. *Costume in Pictures*. New York: F. P. Dutton & Co., 1954.

Eaton, Allen. *Handicrafts of New England*. New York: Harper and Row, 1949.

Earle, Alice. *Two Centuries of Costume in America*. New York: Macmillan Press, 1903.

Earle, Alice. *Costume of Colonial Times*. New York: Charles Scribner's Sons, 1894.

Evans, Mary. *How to Make Historic American Costumes*. New York: Barnes, 1942.

Hawke, David. *Colonial Experience*. New York: Bobbs-Merrill, 1966.

Kauffman, Henry. *The Colonial Silversmith*. New York: Thomas Nelson and Sons, 1969.

Klenke, William W. *Candlemaking*. New York: Manual Press, 1946.

Laklan, Carle. *The Candle Book*. New York: M. Barrows, 1956.

Life, editors. *America's Arts and Skills*. New York: E. P. Dutton & Co., 1957.

Monroe, Ruth. *Kitchen Candlecrafting*. S. Brunswick: A. S. Barnes, 1970.

Sherman, Frederic. *Early Connecticut Artists and Craftsmen*. New York: Privately published, 1925.

Speare, Elizabeth. *Life in Colonial America*. New York: Random House, 1963.

Pamphlets and Magazines:

Foley, David. "Indian and Pilgrim," *Grade Teacher*, 78:20 N, 1960.

Peterson, Harold. *Arms and Armor in Colonial America, 1526–1783*. Harrisburg, Pa.: Stackpole Co., 1956.

Pinshiell, E. W. "Make Pilgrim and Indian Costumes, Then Use Them," *Instructor,* Vol. 70:34.

Films:

"Handicraft I" Danbury High School

"Handicraft II" Danbury High School

"Pilgrims"—Their persecution, life in Holland, crossing to New England. Danbury High School

"Plymouth Colony: The First Year"—Tells events of first year and struggle in establishing freedom. Coronet Films.

"Mayflower Story"—Details of 17th century ship construction, ancient tools used.

"The Light Kindled Here." Scenes of ship handling, sailing, shipboard life of Pilgrims. International Film Bureau.

"The Pilgrims." Pilgrim religious persecution in England, the North Atlantic crossing, first winter here. Danbury High School.

Filmstrips:

"English Background and Voyage to the New World." SVE Filmstrips (53 frames, 14 min.)

"The First Year in the New World." SVE Filmstrips (49 frames, 14 min.)

Slides:

"Plymouth, Mass." Danbury High School. (20-2 x 2 slides)

Pictures and Maps:

A portfolio available through Plymouth Plantation, Plymouth, Massachusetts. To be used for the opaque projector.

SECTION II

FAMOUS AMERICANS

7

Benjamin Franklin's Birthday
January 17, 1706

The question may be asked, "Why Benjamin Franklin? Why not some other famous American?"

Benjamin Franklin's life was one of the more exciting stories in American history. His accomplishments were significant and his sayings so stirring that he seemed just right for a place in a book on special days in the classroom.

Also, so many schools carry the name Benjamin Franklin that it is appropriate to provide teachers with suggestions and guidelines for celebrating his birthday in those schools.

PERTINENT FACTS

Franklin was the first to:

> Suggest daylight saving.
> Create a lending library.
> Plan street lighting.
> Organize a fire-fighting company.
> Start a thrift campaign.
> Devise a plan for uniting the Colonies.
> Recognize that oil can be used to quiet a rough sea.
> Organize an anti-slavery society in this country.
> Encourage education for agriculture, insurance for crops, and chemical fertilizer.
> Establish a foreign-language newspaper in this country.

Organize our postal system.

Start a fire-insurance company.

Publish questions and answers in a newspaper.

Build a hospital in this country.

Organize a street-cleaning system.

Determine the relative absorption of heat by different colors.

Organize a militia in the Province.

Advocate the use of airtight compartments in ships.

Introduce Scotch kale, Chinese rhubarb, Swiss barley and the yellow willow for basket-making.

Predict the use of airborne troops after seeing balloon flight.

Promote silk culture in Pennsylvania.

SUGGESTED CLASSROOM ACTIVITIES

1. Exhibit of Benjamin Franklin "Firsts": A collection by pupils of things, or pictures of them, invented by Franklin, such as his stove, first American cartoon, foreign-language newspaper, etc.

2. Photograph things around the city to which Franklin contributed: libarary, lightning rods, etc. Exhibit pictures at school.

3. Make an Almanac after the manner of Poor Richard's. Have it mimeographed and circulated through the school.

4. Put out a Franklin issue of the school paper, imitating his *Gazette.*

5. Each week, put a Franklin quotation or Poor Richard saying on the bulletin board as the slogan of the week.

6. Give a play or pageant. Make Franklin posters.

7. Hold an information quiz on Benjamin Franklin and his time.

8. Make an effort to have every boy and girl deposit in the school savings system during National Thrift Week.

9. For younger children, a game of charades acting out a Franklin adage.

10. Shadowgraphs are fun. Act out some incidents in Franklin's life behind a sheet with a light behind the actors.
11. Simple Franklin experiments in science could be demonstrated by the Science Club, such as ringing a bell with electricity, heat absorption by different colors, cooling by evaporation, etc.
12. Read selections aloud from Franklin's *Autobiography*.
13. Make art or paper costumes of the Franklin period.
14. Show movies of Franklin's life.
15. Highlight his role in the American Revolution or in government, using a skit, panel discussion, question games, or small-group work.
16. Hold an essay contest on such topics as Franklin the inventor, the author, the diplomat. The best papers or excerpts can be reprinted in the school paper.
17. Reproduce Franklin's *Gazette*.
18. Discuss *Poor Richard's Almanac*.
19. Read and analyze one of his essays.
20. Follow his travels during a given period of his life.
21. Report on a book dealing with his life.
22. Write an analysis of his wit and humor.
23. Make a bust of Franklin.

SUGGESTED LESSON GUIDELINES

Special Day: BENJAMIN FRANKLIN'S BIRTHDAY

Guideline I

1. Write the name of Benjamin Franklin and the date January 17th on the chalkboard. Ask the students to suggest thoughts and facts they know about this great man and the date written. Start a composite list on the chalkboard.

   Typical responses:
   a. his birthday
   b. inventor
   c. printer

    d. *Poor Richard's Almanac*
    e. Declaration of Independence

2. Commend the group on their knowledge and introduce a thirty-minute film on *The Life of Benjamin Franklin*. Alert them to new feelings and facts they might wish to watch for in the film.

    Typical alerts:
        a. Philadelphia
        b. diplomat
        c. customs
        d. dress of the times
        e. the *Gazette*

3. Include a homework assignment or research assignment: Let's all increase our knowledge by doing some individual research . . . we can share our findings at our next meeting.

    Typical additions:
        a. politics
        b. slogans
        c. science
        d. foreign travel
        e. wit and humor

Guideline II

1. Explore with the class the best way they might learn about Benjamin Franklin and celebrate his birthday on January 17.

    Typical responses:
        a. Let's have a party on his birthday
        b. Make posters and make up slogans
        c. Let's create political cartoons of his time
        d. Let's make a newspaper of his day
        e. Read some of his essays

2. It's obvious that Benjamin Franklin was a great man and has accomplished much more than any one of us will be able to

study by ourselves in such a short time, so I wonder how we can accomplish the most and learn together in this class. Any suggestions?

Typical responses:

    a. We could all take one topic
    b. Work together on the "buddy system"
    c. Look in different source books
    d. Divide into groups
    e. See some more movies

3. If we decided to divide into groups, how could we form them so that we would be fair to everyone in the class and get the most out of our studies?

Typical responses:

    a. Divide by boys and girls (random selection)
    b. Special interest areas (topic)
    c. Balanced ability groups (heterogeneous lines)
    d. Work with our friends (sociometric lines)
    e. Ability groupings (with matching degrees of difficulties)

Guideline III

Here is an opportunity for the teacher to introduce grouping techniques within the classroom and also to draw upon the advantage of group dynamics. Before allowing the youngsters to select the type of group formation they wish to attempt, determine the advantages:

    a. sense of working together, belonging, sharing, security
    b. encourages them to think for themselves
    c. respect for each other's contributions
    d. promotes cooperation
    e. promotes active participation in learning more

First attempts mean that the teacher and student must develop some rules for the group:

Typical rules:

   a. purpose
   b. time period for the study
   c. roles of group membership
   d. conduct rules
   e. reporting and participation rules and grading rules

Typical organization pattern:

   a. chairman: gives directions; keeps them on the subject; prevents fooling; makes sure all participate.
   b. recorder: keeps a daily activity record (as a group we did . . . ; individuals are responsible for . . . ; plans . . .)
   c. observer or evaluator (rotating plan): how many participated? did they stick to the task? work smoothly? are jokers spoiling the project?

Typical reporting activities:

   a. written composite project report with illustrations
   b. oral support, which may include guest speaker
   c. short skit or play depicting the topic.
   d. getting the class involved with worksheets or news clippings
   e. making records, tape recordings, slides, models, charts

Typical grading and/or evaluating:

   a. teacher grades written work
   b. group grades presentation
   c. both individual grades and group grades established

Teacher's role throughout project:

   a. works his way into the background and acts as a resource
   b. suggests "how-to" materials, bibliography materials, etc.
   c. gives some direction if needed

     d. clarifies roles and calls attention to guidelines
     e. circulates among groups

Guideline IV

Provide time for library work and skills, resource people, field trips, community participation, school participation, interdisciplinary participation (art department or teacher, music, printing) . . . provide for reporting and grading on originality, participation, value, etc.

Guideline V

Culmination activities could include written invitations to a birthday party on January 17th, projects, reports, posters, bulletin board illustrations, models, busts, and other recognized contributions. Parents, some teachers, community leaders and the principal could be invited to the party. If possible, the party could be video-taped and a replay could provide a student learning experience.

Guidelines do not represent five working sessions or days. This must be determined by the teacher. It may be weeks or whatever time period the group feels is appropriate.

BIBLIOGRAPHY AND SOURCE MATERIALS
(reading level 4-8)

Adams, *Album of American History*. Scribner, 1944–49.

Adams, *Dictionary of American History*. Scribner, 1940.

American Heritage, *The Many Worlds of Benjamin Franklin*. American Heritage, 1963.

American Heritage, *The Pioneer Spirit*. American Heritage, 1959.

Asimov, Isaac, *The Kite That Won the Revolution*. Houghton-Mifflin, 1963.

Bartlett, *Familiar Quotations*. Little-Brown, 1948.

Benet, *The Reader's Encyclopedia*. Crowell, 1955.

Butterfield, *The American Past*. Simon & Schuster, 1947.

Chamber's Biographical Dictionary. St. Martin's Press, 1961.

Eaton, *That Lively Man, Benjamin Franklin*. Morrow, 1948.

Epstein, *Real Book About Benjamin Franklin*. Garden City Books, 1952.

Harvey, *The Oxford Companion to English Literature*. Oxford, 1958.

Hoyt, *New Cyclopedia of Practical Quotations*. Funk, 1940.

Jameson, *Dictionary of United States History*. Philadelphia Hist. Pub., 1931.

Johnson, Malone, eds., *Dictionary of American Biography*. Scribner, 1928–44.

Kraus, *The United States to 1865*. University of Michigan Press, 1959.

Lincoln Library of Essential Information. Frontier Press, 1924.

McKown, *Benjamin Franklin*. Putnam, 1963.

Meadowcraft, *Benjamin Franklin*. Grosset.

Morris, *Encyclopedia of American History*. Harper, 1961.

Neilson, *Benjamin Franklin*. Row, Peterson, 1950.

Stevenson, Augusta, *Benjamin Franklin: Boy Printer*. Bobbs, 1953.

Webster's Biographical Dictionary. Merriam, 1943.

Wilson, Mitchell, *American Science and Invention*. Simon & Schuster, 1954.

Year, ed., *Pictorial History of America*. Year Inc., 1958.

Join

International Benjamin Franklin Society, 441 Lexington Avenue, New York, N.Y. 10017 ($5.00 yearly).

Filmstrips

"American Leaders" (Benjamin Franklin). McGraw-Hill.
"Ben Franklin of Old Philadelphia." Imperial Film Co.
"Founders of America" (Benjamin Franklin). Encyclopedia Britannica.

Records

"Benjamin Franklin's Autobiography." Scholastic Audio-Visual.

Films

"Benjamin Franklin." Encyclopedia Britannica Films, B/W, 17 min.

8

Lincoln's Birthday
February 12th

Abraham Lincoln, the saviour of his country, the great emancipator, the rail splitter, the boy who walked miles and read by candlelight to seek "book knowledge," the country lawyer who won fame, and the Civil War President of the United States of America who was shot to death while attending a theatre, is probably the most well-known President of the United States. Perhaps many of the tales are exaggerations of the truth; perhaps his honesty and character had many sides; perhaps his position of reverence may be challenged; but, nonetheless, Lincoln provides one of the most thrilling and inspiring areas of study for the classroom. This chapter, then, serves to stimulate and enhance those kinds of actvities, programs and events that add to the educational repertoire of our classroom teachers.

PERTINENT FACTS

1. Born in the state of Kentucky on February 12, 1809, his humble beginnings reflected a meager cabin and an even meaner home life.
2. The cabin was scarcely a hut; the farmland was the roughest sort of a clearing; life was indeed a poverty setting.
3. His father, Thomas Lincoln, was not an ambitious man. He was lazy, could not read, and did not see any use in writing and reading. He was classed as the South's "poor white."
4. His mother, Nancy Hanks, was pretty, could read and write.

It is said that if she had the opportunities of today she could have developed into a beautiful, superior and noble woman.

5. Abraham had a sister, Sarah, and a brother, Thomas.

6. It was Mrs. Lincoln who encouraged Abraham to spell, write and read. He never forgot the goodness and love of his talented mother.

7. Abe liked to play by himself, fish, and although he was not fond of hunting, he did go partridge hunting.

8. When Abe was eight, his father pulled up stakes and moved to Gentryville, Indiana.

9. Abe was growing into manhood, long-legged, spindling, black hair, dreamy-looking eyes, hatchet face, shallow and tanned— not a very nice-looking young boy. He was usually dressed in a raccoon skin hat, deerskin clothing and homespun shirt of cotton.

10. When his mother died in a great epidemic, Abe wrote to his clergyman back in Kentucky asking for a memorial service for her. The next spring a parson did come to preach a funeral sermon.

11. Abe's stepmother turned out to be a blessing for him. She was a hard-working mother who cooked well and encouraged schooling for young Abe.

12. Abe worked hard at splitting rails, ferrying a flatboat across Pigeon Creek, and carrying water. He did farm chores and was a good-natured boy who turned his wages over to his father.

13. At nineteen years of age, Abe became a "bow hand" and went by flatboat down the river to New Orleans.

14. Finally, Abraham and family moved to Illinois in the spring of 1830, where he was to become known as the "rail splitter."

15. He then became a clerk in the New Salem store, where he continued with his "learning."

16. It was in New Salem that Lincoln got his name "Honest Abe."

17. Abraham became a captain in command of the Sangamon company.

18. In 1833 Lincoln became Postmaster of New Salem.

19. In 1834 he was elected to the Legislature by a wide majority. He was twenty-five years of age.

20. In 1840 he married Mary Todd, a Kentucky girl who lived in Springfield.
21. In 1843 he formed the law firm of Lincoln and Herndon.
22. Abe Lincoln became a lawyer in his new home of Springfield, Illinois.
23. He sat as judge in the Circuit Court.
24. In 1854 the famous Lincoln-Douglas debate was a turning point for Abe.
25. In 1858 the new party, called the Republican Party, nominated Abraham Lincoln as Senator from Illinois.
26. The Lincoln-Douglass debate sparked his world-famous speech against slavery, "A house divided against itself cannot stand. . . ."
27. He lost the senatorial race, but in 1860 he was nominated for President of the United States and became President in 1861.
28. The first shot at Fort Sumter, South Carolina, started the Civil War.
29. Lincoln loved the Union, hated slavery, and fought for a free United States of America. In September, 1862, the Emancipation Proclamation was issued.
30. In November, 1863, at Gettysburg, Pennsylvania, President Lincoln made his greatest speech, "Four score and seven years ago our fathers. . . ."
31. In 1865 the Civil War ended with a victory for the Union.
32. On the night of April 14, 1865, John Wilkes Booth shot President Lincoln as he sat watching a play. On April 15, 1865 he closed his eyes forever.

SUGGESTED CLASSROOM ACTIVITIES

1. Write a short story on "Abe Lincoln from country boy to President."
2. Divide the periods of Lincoln's life into the following and have small groups make reports upon their selected period:

   a. Early childhood
   b. Growing up
   c. Debates and speeches

      d. Legislator

      e. Lawyer

      f. President

      g. Significant battles of the Civil War

      h. Constitutional impact, and have interest groups develop the theme for a classroom report.

3. Develop famous sayings and suggest their meaning for us in today's society.

4. Develop role-playing scenes in which Lincoln played an important role.

5. Make illustrations of the times.

6. Select illustrations from source materials and elaborate on the scenes.

7. Make a map of the 1800's and trace Lincoln's growth by depicting monuments, cabins, White House, etc.

8. List and elaborate on the greatest accomplishments of Lincoln.

9. Correlate instructional program with other departments and subjects such as art, music of the period, scientific development of the period, literature, poems, and the influence these had on public opinion during the 1850-1865 period.

10. What economic impact did Lincoln's policies have on the South?

11. What influence did Lincoln have on North-South relations?

12. Make models or transparencies of major events during Lincoln's time.

13. Project what might have happened if the South won the war.

14. Make oral reports on:

      a. Birthplace and Childhood

      b. Lincoln's Education

      c. His Marriage and Family

      d. Dred Scott Decision

      e. Missouri Compromise

      f. Lincoln's Election

      g. Emancipation Proclamation

      h. Trent Affair

    i. Assassination
    j. Ulysses S. Grant
    k. Robert E. Lee
    l. Reconstruction Period

SAMPLE LESSON PLANS

First Day

General background on the life of Abraham Lincoln (1809-1865).

Suggested Teaching Goals:

1. To acquaint pupils with basic facts about Abraham Lincoln.
2. To instill in them the qualities of Lincoln such as kindness, honesty, mercy, brotherhood, courage, and self-betterment.
3. To depict the differences and similarities in the 19th century of Lincoln as compared to the present day.
4. To portray Lincoln as a living image, not as a history book figure to be forgotten.
5. To show pupils the different aspects of Lincoln's life, such as boyhood and education, and compare their own experiences to his.
6. To give the students additional practice in the presentation of oral reports.

Teacher Preparation:

1. Gathering of available reading material to be displayed in the classroom for the students' benefit.
2. Mimeographing a list of library books on Lincoln for each student. These books may be located in the school or public library.
3. Locating illustrations of Lincoln, his family, home, school, documents, etc., for the students to view to form a visual image in their minds.
4. Reading outside sources to refresh the teacher's memory of

Abraham Lincoln in order to put across an interesting yet educational account.

5. Locating audio-visual aids to supplement the lesson.
6. Mimeographing notes on the topics to be discussed throughout the week so that the pupils will be aware of what is to be discussed prior to the lesson and be prepared for discussion.

Audio-Visual Aids Needed:

1. Motion Picture entitled "Lincoln Heritage Trail" (16mm, Sound, 28 minutes).
2. Illustrations of
   a. Abraham Lincoln
   b. His family
   c. Lincoln's birthplace within Lincoln Memorial Building, Hodgenville, Kentucky
   d. Clothing of the era
   e. Lincoln's Tomb in Oak Ridge Cemetery, Springfield, Illinois
   f. Lincoln Memorial, Potomac Park, Washington, D. C.
   g. Emancipation Proclamation
   h. Lincoln-Douglas Debates
   i. Civil War
3. Library books.

Suggested Procedure:

1. Discussion
   a. Why is Lincoln's Birthday a major celebrated holiday?
   b. Lincoln's birth and early childhood
      1) Log cabin—Hodgenville, Kentucky
   c. Young Manhood
      1) Athlete
      2) Education
      3) Occupation
      4) Soldier
   d. Politics and Law Career
      1) Election to state legislature

         2) Study of law
    e. Marriage and Family
         1) Wife: Mary Todd
         2) Children:
            a) Robert Todd
            b) Edward Baker
            c) William Wallace
            d) Thomas (Tad)
    f. Lincoln in Congress
    g. Campaigns
         1) Political party
         2) Lincoln-Douglas debates
         3) Presidential election
2. Motion Picture
3. Oral Reports:
    a. Birthplace and childhood
    b. Education
    c. Marriage and Family
    d. Law Career
    e. Politics
4. Question and answer period on topics discussed and motion picture viewed.
5. Review.

Second Day

Re-enactment of the Lincoln-Douglas Debates.

Suggested Teaching Goals:

1. To help pupils acquire the basic skills and methods of debating.
2. To help them attain cooperation and develop teamwork among their peers.
3. To learn the virtue of good sportsmanship—to be a good winner or loser.
4. To help them develop the proper procedure of presenting one's point of view courteously and defending it.

5. To help them gain knowledge of Lincoln's position on political issues and his opponent's political views.

Pupil Activities:

1. Selection of two teams of five students each to partake in debating teams. One team for the Lincoln presentation and rebuttal, and one for Douglas.
2. Group planning for presentations as an outside activity.
3. Oral reports on:
   a. Lincoln's issues
   b. Douglas' issues
   c. Dred Scott Decision
   d. Missouri Compromise

Teacher Preparation:

1. Gather pictures of the debates.
2. Read outside sources on the proper procedures of debate.
3. Mimeograph pertinent facts on the Lincoln-Douglas debates to be given to the students prior to the lesson for review and study.
4. Locate audio-visual aids to supplement the lesson.

Third Day

Suggested Teaching Goals:

1. To acquaint the pupils with the events that led to the Civil War.
2. To inform the pupils of the major battles of importance.
3. To give the pupils an unbiased account of both sides, the North's and the South's, so that they may form their own convictions.
4. To compare the scale of the Civil War with that of modern wars.
5. To show the ill effects of war and the necessity for a peaceful coexistence.
6. To encourage the qualities of peacefulness, friendliness, and cooperation in the classroom as opposed to the friction of war.

Pupil Activities:

1. Reading material on the Civil War in textbook.
2. Oral reports on:
   a. Ulysses S. Grant
   b. Robert E. Lee
   c. Major battles
   d. Surrender
   e. Reconstruction Period
   f. Outcomes of the War
3. Discussion of Civil War
   a. Causes
   b. Secession of the states
   c. Election of Jefferson Davis as Southern President
   d. War
      1) Generals
         a) Grant
         b) Lee
         c) Sherman
         d) Sheridan
         e) Stonewall Jackson
         f) Pierre Gustave Toutant de Beauregard
      2) Major Battles
         a) Bull Run
         b) Fredericksburg
         c) Gettysburg
         d) Chattanooga
         e) Sherman's March
         f) Appomattox
      3) Politics during the War
         a) Election of Davis
         b) Re-election of Lincoln
      4) Reconstruction Period
4. Filmstrip on Civil War activity
5. Oral Reports
6. Question and Answer Period

Fourth Day

Panel Discussion of Lincoln in Today's World

Suggested Teaching Goals:

1. To instill in pupils an image of Lincoln the man.
2. To gain knowledge of social problems in Lincoln's day as compared to those of today.
3. To make comparisons (open) between President Lincoln and our current president.
4. To depict Lincoln as a living personality in today's affairs.
5. To enhance pupil participation and ease in oral discussion.
6. To have the pupils discover the multiple reasons for celebrating Lincoln's Birthday.

Activities:

1. Panel discussion on Lincoln in today's era. Various topics that could be discussed are:
   a. How would Lincoln handle the Vietnam War?
   b. What would he do to settle student unrest and strikes?
   c. How would he combat air pollution?
   d. What would he do about the increasing rate of unemployment?
   e. What effect would Lincoln have on racial affairs today?
   f. How do the present-day racial problems compare to those in Lincoln's time?
   g. Will a war such as the Civil War occur in this generation due to this racial imbalance?
   h. How would Lincoln promote conservation measures to restore the natural beauty of America?
   i. In what ways are President Lincoln and our current president similar or dissimilar in mannerisms and policies?
   j. Is the Republican Party that sponsored Lincoln basically the same as that of our day?
   k. If you were President, how would you handle these problems?
   l. Was Lincoln as important to world affairs and his countrymen as today's president is?

BIBLIOGRAPHY

Angle, Paul M. *The Lincoln Reader.*

Angle, Paul M., and Miers, Earl S. *The Living Lincoln.*

Barton, William. *Great Good Man.*

Basler, Roy, ed. *Abraham Lincoln: His Speeches and Writings.*

Basler, Roy. *The Lincoln Legend: A Study in Changing Conceptions.*

Bishop, Jim. *The Day Lincoln Was Shot.*

Bruce, Robert. *Lincoln and the Tools of War.*

Catton, Bruce. *Mr. Lincoln's Army.*

Charnwood, Lord. *Abraham Lincoln.*

Cottrel, John. *Anatomy of an Assassination.*

Daugherty, James. *Abraham Lincoln.*

Bisenschiml, Otto. *Why Was Lincoln Murdered?*

Harper, Robert S. *Lincoln and the Press.*

Hendrick, Burton. *Lincoln's War Cabinet.*

Jaffa, Harry. *Crisis of House Divided: Interpretation of Lincoln-Douglas Debates.*

Johnson, R. U., and Buel, C. C. *Battles and Leaders of the Civil War.*

Kenneth, P. *Lincoln Finds a General.*

Kerner, Fred. *A Treasury of Lincoln's Quotations.*

Kingdon, Frank. *Architects of the Republic.*

Latham, Frank. *Lincoln and the Emancipation Proclamation.*

Lewis, Lloyd. *Myths After Lincoln.*

Mearns, David. *The Lincoln Papers.*

Meserve, Frederick, and Sandburgh, Carl. *The Photographs of Abraham Lincoln.*

Mitgang, Herbert. *Lincoln As They Saw Him.*

Morse, John. *Abraham Lincoln.*

Newman, Ralph. *Lincoln for the Ages.*

Patrick, Rembert. *Jefferson Davis and His Cabinet.*

Pratt, Harry. *The Personal Finances of Abraham Lincoln.*

Quarles, Benjamin. *The Negro in the Civil War.*

Randall, James. *The Civil War and the Reconstruction.*

Randall, James. *Lincoln the President.*

Randall, James. *Mr. Lincoln.*

Randall, Ruth. *Mary Lincoln: Biography of a Marriage.*

Rogers, Agnes. *Abraham Lincoln.*

Sandburg, Carl. *Abraham Lincoln: The Prairie Years.*

Sandburg, Carl. *Abraham Lincoln: The War Years.*
Sparks, Edwin. *The Lincoln-Douglas Debates of 1858.*
Thomas, Benjamin. *Abraham Lincoln: A Biography.*
Washington, John. *They Knew Lincoln.*
Wellman, Paul. *The House Divided.*
Williams, T. *Lincoln and His Generals.*
Williams, T. *Lincoln and the Radicals.*
Woldman, Albert. *Lawyer Lincoln.*

9

Dr. Martin Luther King's Day
January 15th

Today it is vital that all teachers be aware of the growing need to commemorate days of famous *contemporary* leaders who have given so much for their country. In some cases their contributions have taken abuse; in other cases the abuse has taken the form of physical threats. Others have gone to jail or appealed to the courts, and some have given their lives for what they believed was right for society.

The recognition of Martin Luther King's birthday is becoming accepted, not only in respect for King as a leader of the black community, but also for his contribution as a humanitarian and fighter for human rights.

Unlike holidays mandated through regular governmental process, the more formal recognition of King's birthday resulted from a "grass roots" movement, in great part generated by students themselves. For example, school closings often resulted from pressure by student groups, or from those who demanded immediate recognition of King.

PERTINENT FACTS

1. Martin Luther King, Jr., an American clergyman, was born in Atlanta, Georgia, in 1929. He was graduated from Morehouse College in 1948 with a B.A. (Bachelor of Arts)

degree. In 1951 he received a B.D. (Bachelor of Divinity) degree from Crozer Theological Seminary. Boston University granted him a Ph.D. (Doctor of Philosophy) degree in 1955. He was ordained in 1947, and in 1954 became minister of a Baptist church in Montgomery, Alabama. King led the boycott in 1955-56 by Montgomery blacks against the segregated city bus lines, and he attained national prominence by advocating a policy of passive resistance to segregation. On December 21, 1956 he gained a major victory and prestige as a black leader when the Montgomery buses began to operate on a desegregated basis. (In 1960 and 1962 he was arrested for leading antidiscrimination demonstrations, but was subsequently released.) In 1964 King was awarded the world-renowned and coveted Nobel Peace Prize. (Shortly before his death in 1968, King was involved in urging a draft boycott by calling upon draft-age Americans, white or black, to boycott the Vietnamese War by declaring themselves conscientious objectors.) He also sought signatures for a peace petition to be presented to President Johnson. Also, in 1967 he called for a civil disobedience drive in northern cities and urged blacks to repudiate the Vietnamese War by supporting a peace candidate in 1968. His untimely death by the bullet of an assassin left an irreplaceable void in leadership for those causes which he espoused and for which he fought. Therefore, the world, in recognition of the late Martin Luther King's leadership in the fight for civil and human rights in America and throughout the world, observes his birthdate on January 15.

2. Received the Pearl Plafknew award for scholarship, 1951.
3. In 1956 was selected as one of the outstanding personalities of the year.
4. In 1963 was named "Man of the Year" by *Time* Magazine.
5. Recipient of the Nobel Peace Prize in 1964.
6. President of the Southern Christian Leadership Conference.
7. Pastor, Dexter Avenue Baptist Church in Montgomery, Alabama.

8. Membership in NAACP, Alpha Phi Alpha, Sigma Pi Phi, Elks.
9. Author of *Stride Toward Freedom,* 1958, and *Why We Can't Wait,* 1964.
10. Advocate of nonviolence marches and demonstrations.
11. A major proponent of the 1964 Civil Rights Act.
12. Married to Coretta Scott King; father of four children, Bunny, Dexter, Marty, and Yoki.
13. 1960, Dr. King and about 75 Atlanta students organized a protest sit-in at Atlanta's richest department store against restaurant and counter-service discrimination.
14. April 2, 1963, Birmingham Lunch Counter protest started by Dr. King. This victory cracked the whole edifice of Southern discrimination.
15. A conference was held with other prominent black leaders to organize the Washington, D.C. "Jobs and Freedom" march on August 28, 1963. Some of those participating were:
    a. A. Philip Randolph of the Brotherhood of Sleeping Car Porters
    b. John Lewis of SNCC
    c. Roy Wilkins of NAACP
    d. Dorothy Height of the National Council of Negro Women
    e. James Farmer of CORE
    f. Whitney Young of the Urban League.
16. At the Washington, D.C. demonstration, Dr. King made his famous speech to over 250,000 spectators: "To Have a Dream." He said:

I say to you today, even though we face the difficulties of today and tomorrow, I still have a dream. It is a dream that is deeply rooted in the American dream. I have a dream that one day this nation will rise up, live out the true meaning of its creed: "We hold these truths to be self-evident, that all men are created equal."
I have a dream that one day on the red hills of Georgia the sons of former slaves and the sons of former slave owners will be able to sit down together at the table of brotherhood. I have

a dream that one day even the state of Mississippi, a state sweltering with people's injustices, sweltering with the heat of oppression, will be transformed into an oasis of freedom and justice.

I have a dream that my four little children one day will live in a nation where they will not be judged by the color of their skin but by the content of their character.

When we allow freedom to ring from every town and every hamlet, from every state and every city, we will be able to speed up that day when all of God's children, black men and white men, Jews and Gentiles, Protestants and Catholics, will be able to join hands and sing in the words of the old Negro spiritual, "free at last!"

As King ended his speech, there was the awed silence that is the very greatest tribute an orator can be paid. And then came a tremendous crash of sound as 250,000 people shouted in ecstatic accord with his words. The feeling that they had of oneness and unity was complete. They kept on shouting in one thunderous voice, and for that brief moment the Kingdom of God seemed to have come on earth.

Life, September 12, 1969.

17. Dr. Martin Luther King graduated from Morehouse College, Georgia.
18. Dr. Martin Luther King was assassinated on April 4, 1968, in Memphis, Tennessee.
19. Dr. King was greatly influenced by Mohandas K. Gandhi, who wrote in 1929:

Let not the 12 million Negroes be ashamed of the fact that they are the grandchildren of slaves. There is no dishonor in being slaves. There is dishonor in being slave owners. But let us not think of honor or dishonor in connection with the past. Let us realize that the future is with those who would be truthful, pure and loving. For, as the old wisemen have said, Truth ever is, untruth never was, love alone binds and truth and love accrue only to the truly honorable.

20. On March 7, 1955, King's lieutenants and John Lewis of SNCC began the famous Selma-to-Montgomery march.
21. Dr. King received an honorary degree from Yale University in New Haven, Conn., and was cited by its president, Kingman Brewster, Jr., as follows:

> When outrage and shame together shall one day have vindicated the promise of legal, social and economic opportunity for all citizens, the gratitude of people everywhere and of generations of Americans yet unborn will echo our admiration.

SUGGESTED CLASSROOM ACTIVITIES

1. Review the facts, conditions under which he **was** arrested, and situation of one of Dr. King's arrests, and have an imaginary "confrontation." Have the group decide on issues, moral values, and fairness.
2. Conduct a mock trial.
3. Provide the students with enough information to have a short skit.
4. Use a camera and cassette tape recorder to interview local black and political leaders.
5. Show the film, *Frederick Douglas,* and discuss the "fathers" of civil rights movements.
6. Present the most recent history of the nonviolence movement.
7. Discuss men of peace and tape a session or two.
8. Review the "To Have a Dream" speech. Have students interpret it and its relationship to King's movement.
9. Arrange appropriate and creative bulletin board and display case arrangements.
10. Video tape candid shots or clips of situations that exemplify brotherhood.
11. Have students write essays on:
    a. Brotherhood practiced throughout the year
    b. Brotherhood is every day, everywhere.
12. Arrange an appropriate book display and have students report on individual books.

13. Rehearsal for play (in action) or excerpt from play and discuss its underlying message.

14. Art displays of famous black men and women and their contributions.

15. Choral rehearsals of civil rights songs.

16. Physical Education classes depicting working, learning, and playing together.

17. Have pupils work on African art, with explanation and interpretation.

18. Teacher's anecdotal forms may be appropriate.

19. Discuss cafeteria scenes that demonstrate brotherhood.

20. Review groups such as Scouts, cheerleaders; sports activities showing cooperation.

21. Interviews: students, principals, teachers, on relevant topics.

22. Students leaving school or entering may be captains for classroom discussion.

23. Black crossing guards helping white children can be used to tell a story.

24. Dancing and drama may discover black musical contributions.

25. Sing "It's a Small World."

26. Develop a slide-showing of such areas as Biafra, Nigeria, Tanzania, and consider their contributions to our American culture.

27. Discuss the message of such books as *Soul on Ice, New Negro Poets, I Am the Darker Brother, Poetry of the Negro,* and *Black Rage.*

28. Spanish classes may wish to discuss *Estevanico,* a famous black Spaniard.

29. Class discussion of equal job opportunities, earning power and what it means to all people.

30. A Speech for all Students: [1]

Topic: A speech of eulogy, eulogizing Dr. Martin Luther King.
Objective: 1) To commemorate the life of a great man.
                   2) Learn how to give a speech of eulogy.
Motivation: 1) January 15 proclaimed day of observance.

---

[1] Suggested by Estella Metviner, Norwalk, Conn. Public Schools.

2) King was winner of the Nobel Peace Prize.
3) He was a leader in the fight for civil and human rights.

Method: 1) Pupils will deliver a 3- to 5-minute speech eulogizing Dr. Martin Luther King.
  a) Extemporaneous speech with use of an outline on a 3 x 5 card.
  b) Speech rating sheet to be utilized by fellow students (see following sample).

SPEECH RATING SHEET [2]

Skills	Score			Comments
	Unsatisfactory	Satisfactory	Excellent	
Presence				Ease, audience contact, bearing, posture, gestures
Vocabulary				Pronunciation, usage
Articulation				Distinctness, substitutions, omissions, additions, consonant faults, vowel faults
Voice				Support, clarity, pitch level, flexibility, resonance, strength
Reading				Stress, phrasing, intonation, rate

General Estimate

Date _____ Grade

[2] *Voice and Diction Handbook,* by L. Levy, E. W. Mammer, R. Sonkin, Prentice-Hall, Inc., 1950.

BIBLIOGRAPHY

Books

Ahmann, Mathew H., ed. *The New Negro.* Notre Dame, Ind.: Fides, 1961.

Bennett, Lerone, Jr. *What Manner of Man: A Biography of Martin Luther King, Jr.* Chicago: Johnson Publishing Co., 1964; 1968.

Brooks, C. U., and Trout, L. *I've Got a Name.* Level I. New York: Holt, Rinehart and Winston, undated.

Clark, Bennett B., ed. *The Negro Protest.* Boston: Beacon, 1963.

Hamilton, Michael P., ed. *The Vietnam War: Christian Perspectives.* Grand Rapids: Eerdmans, 1967.

Harcourt, Melville, ed. *Thirteen for Christ.* New York: Sheed and Ward, 1963.

King, Martin Luther, Jr. *The Measure of a Man.* Philadelphia: United Church Press, 1958.

King, Martin Luther, Jr. *Strength to Love.* New York: Harper and Row, 1963.

King, Martin Luther, Jr. *Stride Toward Freedom: The Montgomery Story.* New York: Harper and Row, 1958.

King, Martin Luther, Jr. *The Trumpet of Conscience.* New York: Harper and Row, 1968.

King, Martin Luther, Jr. *Where Do We Go from Here: Chaos or Community?* New York: Harper and Row, 1967.

King, Martin Luther, Jr. *Why We Can't Wait.* New York: Harper and Row, 1964.

Lomax, Louise E. *To Kill a Blackman.* Los Angeles: Holloway House, 1968.

Miller, William Robert. *Martin Luther King, Jr.: His Life. Martyrdom and Meaning for the World.* New York: Weybright and Talley, 1968.

Murray, A., and Thomas, R. *The Journey.* New York: Scholastic Book Services, 1970.

Peck, Ira. *The Life and Words of Martin Luther King.* New York: Scholastic Book Services, 1970.

Reddick, Lawrence D. *Crusader Without Violence: A Biography of Martin Luther King, Jr.* New York: Harper and Row, 1959.

Articles

Abernathy, Ralph D. "My Last Letter to Martin." *Ebony* (July, 1968).

Baldwin, James. "The Dangerous Road before Martin Luther King." *Harper's* (February, 1961).

Bennett, John C. "Martin Luther King, Jr., 1929–1968." *Christianity and Crisis* (April 15, 1968).

Bosmajian, Haig A. "Rhetoric of Martin Luther King's Letter from Birmingham Jail." *Midwest Quarterly,* Vol. VIII (January, 1967).

Cleaver, Eldridge. "Requiem for Nonviolence." *Ramparts* (May, 1968).

Cleghorn, Reese. "Martin Luther King, Jr., Apostle of Crisis." *Saturday Evening Post* (June 15, 1963).

Cook, Bruce. "King in Chicago." *Commonweal* (April 29, 1966).

Cowan, Wayne H. "Selma at First Hand." *Christianity and Crisis* (April 5, 1965).

Galphin, Bruce M. "Political Future of Dr. King." *The Nation* (September 23, 1961).

Garland, Phyl. "I've Been to the Mountaintop." *Ebony* (May, 1968).

Halberstam, David. "The Second Coming of Martin Luther King." *Harper's* (August, 1967).

Harding, Vincent. "The Religion of Black Power." *The Religious Situation,* 1968, ed. Donald R. Cutler. Boston: Beacon Press, 1968.

King, Coretta. "How Many Men Must Die?" *Life* (April 19, 1968).

King, Martin Luther, Jr. "Dreams of Brighter Tomorrows." *Ebony* (March, 1965).

Lincoln, C. Eric. "Weep for the Living Dead." *The Christian Century* (May 1, 1968).

Maguire, John David. "Martin Luther King and Vietnam." *Christianity and Crisis* (May 1, 1967).

Maguire, John David. "Martin Luther King, Jr., 1929–1968." *Christianity and Crisis* (April 15, 1968).

Meier, August. "On the Role of Martin Luther King." *New Politics,* Vol. IV (Winter, 1965).

Meyer, Frank S. "Principles and Heresies." *National Review* (April 20, 1965).

Miller, Perry. "The Mind and Faith of Martin Luther King." *The Reporter* (October 30, 1958.).

Parks, Gordon. Untitled article. *Life* (April 19, 1968).

Pitcher, Alvin. "Martin Luther King Memorial." *Criterion,* Vol. VII, No. 2 (Winter, 1968).

Rose, Stephen C. "Epitaph for an Era." *Christianity and Crisis* (June 10, 1963).

Rowan, Carl T. "Martin Luther King's Tragic Decision." *Reader's Digest* (September, 1967).

Sharma, Mohan Lal. "Martin Luther King: Modern America's Greatest Theologian of Social Action." *Journal of Negro History,* Vol. LIII (July, 1968).

Tallmer, Jerry. "Martin Luther King, Jr., His Life and Times." *New York Post,* April 8, 1968.

Additional information relating to Dr. King can be obtained from:

Southern Christian Leadership Conference
Montgomery, Alabama

Martin Luther King Memorial Center
Spelman College
Atlanta, Georgia

SECTION III
ETHNIC CONTRIBUTIONS

10
Black History Week (*February*) and a Unit on Minority Groups in America

Students must have opportunities to recognize the multi-ethnic nature of our nation. Until recently, attention to minority groups primarily involved those who came to our shores from Europe or the Orient, beginning about 1840. The rich contributions of the influx of these peoples have long been recognized as the basic fiber of America. However, we have unfortunately neglected one important segment of our society: the black American.

This chapter provides the kind of information necessary for developing a meaningful awareness, first, of the contributions of the black American and, second, of the role and history of minority groups in general.

We begin with a summary of the black American's progress during the past thirty years; for it has been during that period that the black American has begun to truly move beyond second-class citizenship. We will also trace the progress and traditions of minority groups other than the black. Throughout the chapter we will experience opportunities for recognizing and, indeed, evaluating our own attitudes about ourselves and our relationships with our fellow Americans. This is particularly essential for us as Americans; for we, in fact, each to some degree, represent some minority group.

**A Summary of the Black American's Progress
During the Past Thirty Years** [1]

1941   First class of black pilots graduated from segregated
        aviation school at Tuskegee Army Air Field, March 7.

        Robert C. Weaver becomes director of a section in the
        Office of Production Management devoted to integrat-
        ing blacks into national defense program, April 18.

        Black seaman Dorie Miller shoots down six of the Jap-
        anese bombers attacking Pearl Harbor, December 7.
        Receives Navy Cross, May 27, 1942.

        President Franklin D. Roosevelt issues Executive Order
        8802, providing for anti-discrimination clauses in all
        defense contracts and establishing a Fair Employment
        Practices Commission in the Office of Production Man-
        agement, June 25.

        A threatened march on Washington by blacks led to
        the first federal Fair Employment Practices Commis-
        sion.

        Dr. Charles Drew develops the blood bank system in
        United States and England.

1942   All-black 332nd Fighter Group activated under the
        command of black Colonel Benjamin O. Davis, Jr., in
        October. During the war, the Group flew 1,579 mis-
        sions, destroyed 260 enemy planes, damaged 148
        others, and sank a German destroyer. Ninety-five of its
        pilots awarded Distinguished Flying Cross.

        Congress of Racial Equality (CORE) begins its career
        of protest in Chicago.

1943   Dr. James C. Evans becomes an official of U.S. War
        Department.

---

[1] From "The Role of the Black in American History Curriculum Guide,"
Norwalk Public Schools, Norwalk, Conn., 1968, based upon *A Layman's Guide to
Negro History,* ed. by Erwin A. Salk, McGraw-Hill Book Co., N.Y., 1967. Director
of Intergroup Programs, Barbara Littlejohn.

In spring of 1943, the most violent of civilian clashes exploded in Detroit, a center for war industries that had attracted many Southern blacks and whites. Federal troops had to be called in.

1944   In Smith v. Allwright, U.S. Supreme Court rules the all-white primary election unconstitutional.

In Morgan v. Virginia, U.S. Supreme Court reverses the conviction of a black passenger who violated Virginia's segregation laws by not vacating a bus seat, citing need for uniformity in the regulation of interstate commerce.

All-black 92nd Infantry Division loses 3,000 lives in Italian Campaign. Awarded 65 Silver Stars, 162 Bronze Stars, and 1,300 Purple Hearts.

In April—a black gun crew aboard the U.S. Intrepid won the Bronze Star for bringing down Japanese Kamakazis.

Adam Clayton Powell elected to Congress as first black Representative from the East.

1945   New York becomes the first to pass a state F.E.P.C.

Ebony magazine made first appearance. This magazine contained stories emphasizing the achievement and success of blacks.

1946   President Truman appoints William Hastie Governor of Virgin Islands.

President Truman created Committee on Civil Rights.

1947   Jackie Robinson, first black American in major league baseball, played with the Brooklyn Dodgers.

CORE—during summer picketed against the segregated swimming pool at Palisades Park, New Jersey, and finally won.

1948   President Truman appoints Dr. James C. Evans to supervise desegregation of the military establishment.

President Truman issued Executive Order 9981, which banned racial discrimination in the armed forces.

Ralph Bunche became Acting Mediator for the United States in Palestine.

1949   Wesley A. Brown became first black graduate of Annapolis Naval Academy.

William Hastie was appointed judge of United States Circuit Court of Appeals.

Connecticut became first state to ban discrimination in housing.

1950   In McLaurin v. Board of Regents, U.S. Supreme Court rules against classroom and social segregation of black student attending University of Oklahoma.

In Sweat v. Painter, U.S. Supreme Court rules that equality of education entails more than comparability of facilities, implying that "separate," by definition, must be unequal.

In Henderson v. United States, U.S. Supreme Court strikes down Interstate Commerce Commission ruling requiring black passengers in railroad dining cars to eat behind a partition.

Gwendolyn Brooks becomes only black woman to receive Pulitzer Prize, May 1.

Ralph J. Bunche becomes first black American to receive Nobel Peace Prize, September 22.

All-black 24th Infantry Regiment scores first victory of Korean conflict at Yechon, July 20.

Edward Dudley served as minister to Liberia.

President Truman appointed Mrs. Edith Sampson as alternate delegate to the United Nations for the United States.

1951   While important progress had been made toward securing equality in America, both silent and open opposition to black advancement continued. On Christmas night, Harry T. Moore and his wife were killed by a bomb placed beneath their Florida home. Both had been leaders in the drive of the state NAACP to register more blacks to vote.

1952   Tuskegee Institute reported that for the first time in 71 years, there were no lynchings.

1954   In Brown v. Board of Education, Supreme Court rules that "separate educational facilities are inherently unequal," striking down the ruling in Plessy v. Ferguson. This decision reversed a half century of legal segregation.

Washington, D.C., Wilmington, St. Louis, and Baltimore begin school desegregation.

Benjamin O. Davis became first black general in the U.S.A.F.

1955   Interstate Commerce Commission orders the end of segregation in interstate travel.

Mrs. Rosa Parks refuses to vacate her bus seat, sparking the black boycott of Montgomery, Alabama bus system, December 1.

A. Phillip Randolph and Willard Townsend become vice presidents of the newly merged AFL-CIO.

Marian Anderson made her Metropolitan Opera debut in Verdi's *Masked Ball.* First black to sing with the company.

1956   Seventy-seven Representatives and nineteen Senators issue "Southern Manifesto" questioning legality of the Supreme Court's ruling and defying its order to desegregate.

U.S. Supreme Court extends principles of Brown decision to higher education in ruling on Florida, ex. rel. Hawkins v. Board of Control.

John H. Sengstacke launches *The Chicago Daily Defender,* one of the nation's two black daily newspapers.

Federal district court rules that segregation on public transportation violates both "due process" and "equal protection" provisions of the Fourteenth Amendment.

Montgomery, Alabama desegregates its entire public transportation system, December.

Rev. Glen Smiley, white minister, rode with Dr. Martin Luther King to integrate Alabama buses.

1957   Congress passes Civil Rights Act of 1957, August 29. The 1957 Act establishes the United States Commission on Civil Rights as a temporary, independent, bipartisan agency. It also made provisions to protect and strengthen the voting rights of all American citizens.

Federal troops ordered to Little Rock, Arkansas, to facilitate desegregation of Central High School.

Dr. Martin Luther King and other black leaders form the Southern Christian Leadership Conference.

Althea Gibson became women's tennis champion.

1958   Dr. Ralph J. Bunche becomes Undersecretary of the United Nations.

1960   President Eisenhower signs Civil Rights Act of 1960, May 6. The 1960 Act provides greater protection of voting rights and makes it a crime to damage property and transport or possess explosives for this purpose.

Founding of Student Non-Violent Coordinating Committee (SNCC or "SNICK").

Lunch-counter sit-ins were started in Greensboro, North Carolina by students.

Elijah Muhammed, Black Nationalist leader, called for the creation of a black state.

1961   Robert C. Weaver appointed Administrator of the Housing and Home Finance Agency, February 11.

Clifton R. Wharton becomes U.S. ambassador to Norway, March 9.

James Benton Parsons becomes U.S. District Judge in Chicago, the first black appointed to a Federal District Court in continental United States, August 9.

Thurgood Marshall appointed to Second Circuit's Federal Court of Appeals, September 23.

Interstate Commerce Commission orders an end to segregated facilities in terminal buildings.

CORE Freedom Riders number over a thousand, white and black, in early part of the year. Kennedy Administration provides U.S. marshals for protection.

1962 Black and civil rights workers ask New York and Philadelphia to suspend building projects in which discrimination in hiring is evident. Such pleas, with demonstrations at construction sites, lead to some concessions in hiring and training.

James Meredith, guarded by U.S. marshal, becomes first black man to enroll at University of Mississippi.

President Kennedy issued an Executive Order prohibiting discrimination in federally assisted housing.

1963 In one twelve-week period, 1,412 separate civil rights demonstrations take place.

Martin Luther King, Jr., leads demonstration in Birmingham, Alabama. Protest becomes violent, May 7, when Public Safety Commissioner "Bull" Connor orders fire hoses and dogs to be used against demonstrators.

NAACP Field Secretary, Medgar Evers, assassinated by segregationists, as he enters his home, June 12.

William Moore, black postal employee, shot to death as he staged a one-man "Freedom Walk."

More than a quarter million whites and blacks stage a March on Washington for civil rights, August 28.

Four black girls killed in the bombing of their Birmingham, Alabama, Sunday School, September 15.

John Fitzgerald Kennedy, 35th President of the United States, assassinated in Dallas, Texas, November 22.

Carl Rowan appointed U.S. Ambassador to Norway.

1964   A series of apparently spontaneous riots break out in Northern cities. Among the worst were those in the Harlem and Bedford-Stuyvesant sections of New York City; in Rochester, New York; Jersey City, New Jersey; Philadelphia, Pennsylvania; Dixmoor, Illinois.

Malcolm X announces his split with the Black Muslims and the founding of a new movement based on his theories of Black Nationalism, March 12.

Bodies of three civil rights workers found in a crude grave near Philadelphia, Mississippi, August 4. The boys, two whites and one black, were murdered by white segregationists June 21.

Civil Rights Act, including public accommodations, voter registration and fair employment sections, signed into law by President Lyndon B. Johnson, July 2. Senate imposed cloture to end a Southern filibuster, June 10.

Dr. Martin Luther King, Jr., becomes second black American to win Nobel Peace Prize.

Carl Rowan appointed Director of the United States Information Agency.

Sidney Poitier becomes first black man to win "Oscar" as best actor of the year, April 13.

1965   Malcolm X is shot down, in New York, by three assassins and dies on the same day, February 21. His three murderers were convicted, March 11, 1966. Two of the three were members of the Black Muslim movement.

Several hundred blacks attempt to march from Selma to Montgomery, Alabama, to protest withholding of black voter registration, Sunday, March 7, 1965. They are beaten back by state police with tear gas, bull whips, cattle prods, and clubs.

Unitarian minister James Reeb, in Selma to participate in the march on Montgomery, is fatally beaten by four white men, March 9. He died two days later.

Addressing the nation in behalf of the black cause, President Johnson announces he will submit a voting rights bill to Congress, March 15.

Federal injunction granted, restraining officials from interfering in Selma march, March 17.

Freedom March from Selma to Montgomery, March 21.

White civil rights worker, Mrs. Viola Gregg Liuzzo, murdered by the white segregationists, March 25.

Congress passes Voting Rights Act, August 4. It is signed by President Johnson, August 6. The 1965 Act provides new tools to assure the right to vote and supplements the previous authority granted by the Civil Rights Acts of 1957, 1960, and 1964.

Race riots break out in Watts area of Los Angeles, California. Riots last seven days, from August 11 to August 17. Considered the most serious race riots in America's history.

The McCone Commission delivers its report on the Watts Riots, December 7. The Commission was set up by Governor Pat Brown of California.

Thurgood Marshall appointed Solicitor General of the United States.

Constance Baker Motley becomes president of New York City's Borough of Manhattan.

Benjamin O. Davis gains rank of Lt. General in May and becomes Deputy Commander, U.S. Forces in Korea. Previously served as Director of Manpower and Training in USAF headquarters.

Mrs. Patricia Harris was appointed U.S. Ambassador to Luxembourg.

1966
to
1971

Constance Baker Motley becomes first black woman to be appointed to a Judgeship in a Federal District Court. She is appointed Judge in Federal District Court of New York City, January 25.

James Farmer leaves his post as Director of CORE. Takes position of leadership in the newly formed National Center for Community Action and Education, Inc., February.

Robert C. Weaver becomes first Negro cabinet member. He is appointed by President Johnson head of the newly created Department of Housing and Urban Development, January 17.

Two black senators and nine congressmen elected to the Georgia legislature.

Stokely Carmichael takes over leadership of Student Non-Violent Coordinating Committee (SNCC), and announces policy of "Black Power," a political and economic movement calling for removal of whites from leadership and policy-making positions within the civil rights organizations.

Floyd McKissick, a North Carolina lawyer, becomes National Director of the Congress of Racial Equality (CORE). CORE subsequently joins SNCC in the espousal of "Black Power," and both organizations modify their traditional commitments to "non-violence."

Robert C. Henry elected mayor of Springfield, Ohio. He was the first black to be chief executive of a northern city, or of any American city of substantial size.

Lucius A. Amerson elected sheriff of Macon County (Tuskegee), Alabama. He was the first black to be elected sheriff in the history of the United States.

James Meredith shot while walking from Memphis to Jackson, Tennessee, in an effort to urge Negro voter registration in the South.

Edward Brooke elected United States Senator from Massachusetts.

Thurgood Marshall was appointed to the United States Supreme Court. First black American to serve as Supreme Court Justice.

Dr. Martin Luther King was assassinated in Memphis, Tennessee. Dr. Ralph Abernathy became head of Southern Christian Leadership Conference.

The "Poor People's March" on Washington began.

Civil Rights legislation regarding open housing.

Some Interesting Facts About
Blacks in History [2]

There have been many interesting blacks who have made valuable contributions to the development of the United States. Blacks have been making their mark on the pages of history since the days of Columbus. In observance of Black History Week and to bring you some facts with which you may not be familiar, we have compiled a group of "Did You Know" items.

Did You Know . . .

. . . a black man, Alonzo Pedro Niva, plotted the course for Columbus' first trip to the New World in 1492?

. . . Estabago, a black Spaniard, led the first non-Indian expedition into Arizona and New Mexico?

. . . a black Bostonian, Crispus Attucks, was the first man to be killed in the American Revolution? The year . . . 1770.

---

[2] Reprinted from *Rights, Opportunities Action Reporter,* State of Connecticut, Commission on Human Rights and Opportunities, Vol. III, No. 1, Jan. 1970.

. . . two hundred thousand black soldiers fought for their freedom in the Civil War? Of these, over thirty-seven thousand gave their lives to the cause.

. . . two black cavalry units rescued Teddy Roosevelt during the battle of San Juan Hill in the Spanish-American War?

. . . Matt Henson, a black member of Commodore Perry's North Pole expedition, arrived with equipment and provisions at the Pole two hours before the Commodore in 1909?

. . . two black men, Private Needham Roberts and Sergeant Henry Johnson, were the first Americans to win France's highest wartime honor, the Croix de Guerre, in World War I?

. . . Dorie Miller, a black Navy cook, was the first American hero of World War II, bringing down four Japanese planes at Pearl Harbor?

For more information concerning the place of the black in American history, write the Connecticut Commission on Human Rights and Opportunities, 90 Washington Street, Hartford, Connecticut 06115.

SUGGESTED CLASSROOM ACTIVITIES

1. Video-tape candid shots or clips of situation that exemplify brotherhood.
2. Write short themes or have debate/discussion on Brotherhood Practiced Throughout the Year, Brotherhood Is Every Day, Brotherhood Is Everywhere, Mutual Respect and Dignity.
3. Library or classroom displays showing individual books available.
4. Design a minority group bulletin board theme that has an instructional message.
5. Poster and cut displays.
6. Choral groups in various languages and/or singing minority group show songs.
7. Physical educational activities depicting contributions or dances of specific groups.
8. Making and interpreting various customs and clothing styles.

9. Discussing and relating personal anecdotes.
10. Have a lunch or party in the custom of an ethnic group or extend this to an international luncheon-type activity.
11. Signs and mottos may be made and interpreted by the class.
12. Produce a short, student classroom paper with a contribution by each member of the class.
13. Bring in young guest speakers from various minority groups.
14. Have one group interview a cross-section of community minority group peoples. Learn about traditions and customs that they feel are important to themselves, and to our way of life in general.

MINORITY GROUPS IN THE UNITED STATES OTHER THAN THE BLACK AMERICAN

I. Minority Groups in the United States
   A. Definition—"What is a minority group? Is it really determined by numbers?"
      1. "Term used to describe the particular social position of some people in relation to the rest of the population."
      2. "Those groups that face certain handicaps, that are subject to discrimination, and that are objects of prejudice from most other people."
      3. "Some groups are allowed and encouraged to merge into 'Americans'; these are the majority—those not merged are minorities." Dynamic concept (not fixed, definition changing).
   B. Characteristics that distinguish minority groups today
      1. Race
      2. Nationality
      3. Religion
      4. Language
   C. What are some of these groups?
      1. Religion
         a. Jews 3%. What picture do you see? Your image is most likely not completely religious.

(1) 1654—First settled in New Amsterdam to find freedom; punished in European ghettos

(2) "Whipping Boy," ex-Nazi Germany; genocide

(3) In U.S., social and economic discrimination. Why? Because of jealousy of the Jews' success.

  b. Catholics 22%

    (1) For many years could not vote in New England colonies

    (2) 1800's—Influx of Irish immigrants; they faced hardship and much discrimination.

    (3) Politically—Al Smith was defeated in 1928 presidential election; very dirty, mud-slinging campaign.

      (a) Ku Klux Klan campaigned vs. Smith on the basis of his religion.

      (b) Who was the first Catholic president? Do you think this prejudice still exists? Why do you believe so? Is your feeling based strictly on your own beliefs, or does it express the feeling of the "majority"? ("Majority" may be the key term to pursue further —if deemed so.)

2. Race—What is it?

  a. Dr. Ruth Benedict—"A group of human beings set apart from others by one or more marks of physical difference is a race."

  b. Biological Characteristics

    (1) Three Basic Categories

      (a) Caucasoid—Europe, Near East, North America, as examples of where such type people may be found.

      (b) Mongoloid—Chinese, Japanese, Indians of America, Eskimos

      (c) Negroid—Africa

  c. Is it fairly safe to say that there is not a pure race left, though "branches" of the main three can rightfully be questioned?

    (1) Examples: Hottentots of Africa, Ainu of Japan, and Australian Bushmen

    d. Listing and Presentation of some racial groups
      (1) Blacks—10% of population
      (2) A brief look into their history
        (a) 1619—First brought as indentured servants.
        (b) Revolution, Civil War—Several times it looked as though slavery would be abolished; however, the Midwestern states and territories passed much legislation highly discriminatory toward blacks.
        (c) 1808—Attempt to halt importation did not work. Cotton gin invented and thus hopes of abolition disappeared.
        (d) Dred Scott case—Justice Taney, "Negro has no rights which a white man must respect"—property.
        (e) Civil War Era—Emancipation by 13th, 14th, and 15th Amendments, 1865, 1868, 1870.
        (f) Reconstruction—This period enforced
        [1] Whites felt that the blacks were beginning to challenge them. Thus, carpetbaggers, scalawags took advantage of blacks for their own ends. (Reinforced segregationists' thoughts of blacks' inability to work.)
        (g) 1900–1954—Caste system evolved.
        [1] Caste (complete separation, no social mobility vertically); racial etiquette "sir" vs. "boy."
        (h) 1954—Brown vs. Board of Education
        [1] "Separate but equal is not possible." (Chief Justice Warren's comment could be read, if desired.)
        (i) 1954 to date—Blacks have made some moderate strides, but much still has to be done.
      (3) American Indian—400,000 population
        (a) Most of tribal lands taken from him
        (b) Low level of living on most reservations
        (c) Tuberculosis and infant mortality rates high in comparison to those of whites; life expectancy very low.

(d) Indians caught between two cultures. Teenagers made to feel very uncertain.

(4) Orientals—Chinese and Japanese

(a) Chinese imported as cheap labor; could not maintain high standards of living with low wages, because poverty-stricken, and were disliked by all whites.

[1] 1882—Chinese Exclusion Act—no more immigration. 1970—Now better assimilated.

(b) Japanese—Thrifty; could acquire and develop properties, which other immigrants could not; became middle class but could not shake discrimination.

[1] After Pearl Harbor, war hysteria spread. Military Command ordered removal of Japanese from coastal areas; 110,000 relocated to camps inland, had to abandon property and sell personal effects. Thus, no earning power; lost a great deal. Thirty thousand served in Armed Forces.

3. Nationality—Language

a. What is an ethnic group? Group set off by race, religion, or national origin; "sense of peoplehood."

(1) Immigrants—Two theories—1870–1920

(a) Melting Pot—Out of many diverse cultures comes a uniform American pattern. Almost total assimilation of all cultural traits.

(b) Cultural Pluralism—Various nationalities have much that is fine and worthwhile in their cultures, which ought to be transplanted and cultivated. Once accepted, there would be a less unified cultural nationalism in America—less of a desire to "live like Americans."

(2) Waves of Immigration

(a) 1800's—Irish, Germans, Norwegians, and Northern Europeans

(b) 1890–1920—Southern and Eastern Europeans

(c) Patterns of Assimilation

[1] 1st Generation—"out group"

[2] 2nd Generation—"marginal group"

[3] 3rd Generation—"in group"

   (3) Latest Immigration

      (a) Puerto Rico, 1920 on—Migrants in reality; Spanish-speaking; highly illiterate; high birth rate; lower paying rates; lower paying jobs.

      (b) Mexicans—1.7 million people—Southwestern seasonal farm labor; "stoop labor"; whole family works; no education; called "wetbacks."

      (c) Cesar Chavez, a leader of this group.

II. Review of Previous Day's Lecture

  A. What is your definition of a minority group?

    1. Is that all-inclusive or would someone like to add or delete from it?

  B. Name the four characteristics of a minority group and give an example for each.

  C. What significance does the case of Brown vs. the Board of Education have in the progress of minority groups to find a rightful place in our society?

    1. Is this Supreme Court decision still being tested today?

    2. Can you give me an example of this testing?

    3. Is this "testing" merely sectional or is it national?

  D. Diagram—Melting Pot vs. Cultural Pluralism

    1. Melting Pot—Out of many diverse cultures comes a uniform American pattern. Almost total assimilation of all cultural traits.

    2. Cultural Pluralism—Various nationalities have much that is fine and worthwhile in their cultures, which ought to be transplanted and cultivated. Once accepted, there would be a less unified cultural nationalism in America—less of a desire to "live like Americans."

III. Redefine Prejudice and Discrimination

  A. Prejudice: Opinion or judgement formed before examination of the facts.

  B. Discrimination: Unfair or injurious treatment of people usually because of race, nationality, religion, or sex. (Overhead

material from past lecture may be used.)
IV. Patterns of Discrimination by Majority Group
   A. Physical Force—Not sufficient for effective long-term domi-
      nation (lynching and now bombings).
   B. Regulating Numbers by Means of Quotas
      1. United States. No immigration restrictions until 1882. "Na-
         tive Americans" getting jumpy as more and more immi-
         grants crowded cities.
      2. 1882—Selection Process—No Chinese laborers, defectors
         or paupers, no criminals or prostitutes.
      3. 1921—Policy of Restriction—350,000 allowed in by na-
         tionalities—3% of those in United States in 1910 (few
         Southern and Eastern Europeans).
      4. 1929—Quota computed by national origins; 150,000 al-
         lowed in.
      5. 1952—McCarren-Walter Act—Consolidated all existing
         quotas—First 50% of any quota should have "needed
         skills"—Favored filling quota with relatives of United States
         citizens.
      6. October, 1965—Replaced nationality quotas with prefer-
         ence system.
         a. Families in United States
         b. Possessed needed skills
         Limits: 120,000 from Latin America and Canada, 20,000
            from nations outside Western Hemisphere.

Questions:

   1. Do you think that all people should be allowed into the
      country? Why?
   2. In the case of dropping all quota restrictions, would the fear
      of overpopulation be given serious consideration? How
      densely populated are we in comparison with other coun-
      tries?
   C. Ballot-box (Political)
      1. Poll tax, literacy tests—Not even allowing them to register.

D. Education and Housing
   1. Afraid that property values will decline
   2. Afraid status loss will occur
   3. Civil Rights Act of 1968 seeks to prohibit discrimination in sale or rental of 80% of nation's housing by 1970.
V. Segregationist Thinking
  A. Definition—One who believes in the separation or isolation of a race, class, or ethnic group by enforced or voluntary residence in a restricted area.
VI. Follow-up (Assignment)—mimeographed sheets
VII. Evaluation—What were the patterns of discrimination by majority groups discussed today? What examples can you give for each?
VIII. Review of Major Concepts
  A. Definitions
    1. Minority groups—Those groups that face certain handicaps, that are subject to discrimination and that are objects of prejudice from most other people.
    2. Prejudice—Opinion or judgment formed without taking time and care to judge fairly.
    3. Discrimination—Action or actions that show favoritism for or against certain individuals or groups.
    4. Race—A group of human beings set apart from others by one or more marks of physical difference.
    5. Ethnic Group—Group set off by race, religion, or natural origin.
    6. "Wetbacks"—Mexicans; "Stoop Labor"—Mexican immigrant workers.
    7. Stereotype.
  B. Theories of Assimilation (diagram theories on board)
    1. Melting Pot—Out of many diverse cultures comes a uniform American pattern. Almost total assimilation of all cultural traits.
    2. Cultural Pluralism—Various nationalities have much that is fine and worthwhile in their cultures, which ought to be transplanted and cultivated. Once accepted, there would be

a less unified cultural nationalism in America—less of a desire to "live like Americans."

C. Name and tell a little about the principal minority groups.
D. Patterns of Discrimination
   1. Violence or force
   2. Regulating numbers by means of quotas
   3. Ballot-box (Political)
   4. Education and Housing
   5. Segregationist Thinking
E. Discussion
   1. What can you do about prejudice and discrimination?
   2. What responsibilities do members of minority groups have in winning equal rights?
   3. Are there any questions concerning any portions of this unit?

BIBLIOGRAPHY

Adoff, Arnold. *Black on Black*. Macmillan, 1968.

Aptheker, Herbert, ed. *A Documentary History of the Negro People in the U.S.* Citadel, 1951. Paperback.

Bennett, Lerone. *Before the Mayflower*. Johnson, 1962. Paperback.

Botkin, Benjamin. *Lay My Burden Down*. University of Chicago Press, 1964. Paperback.

Cronan, Edmund. *Black Moses: The History of Marcus Garvey*. University of Wisconsin, 1955.

Davidson, Basil. *Black Mother: The Years of the African Slave Trade*. Little, Brown, 1961.

Davis, Allison W. and Dollard. *Children of Bondage*. Washington: American Council on Education, 1940.

DuBois, W. E. B. *Black Reconstruction in America, 1860-1880*. Meridian, 1962.

DuBois, W. E. B. *The Souls of Black Folk*. Peter Smith, n.d. Paperback.

Essien-Udom, E. U. *Black Nationalism*. Dell, 1962. Paperback.

Franklin, John Hope. *From Slavery to Freedom*. Revised. Knopf, 1956.

Frazier, E. Franklin. *The Negro Church in America*. Schocken, 1963.

Ginzberg, Eli. *The Negro Challenge to the Business Community*. McGraw, 1964. Paperback.

Grant, Joanne, ed. *Black Protest: History, Documents and Analyses*. Fawcett, 1968. Paperback.

Greene, Lorenzo Johnstone. *Negro in Colonial New England*. Atheneum, 1968. Paperback.

Herskovits, Melville. *The New World Negro*. University of Indiana Press, 1966.

Herskovits, Melville. *The Myth of the Negro Past*. Beacon, 1958.

Hiestand, Dale. *Economic Growth and Employment Opportunities for Minorities*. Columbia University Press, 1964.

Johnson, Charles S. *Shadow of the Plantation*. University of Chicago Press, 1965. Paperback.

Kardiner, Abram. *The Mark of Oppression*. Meridian, 1962. Paperback.

Lee, Frank F. *Negro and White in a Connecticut Town*. College and University Press, 1962.

Lewis, Hylan. *Blackways of Kent*. University of North Carolina, 1964.

Lincoln, C. Eric. *The Black Muslims in America.* Beacon, 1961.

Lomax, Louis E. *The Negro Revolt.* New American Library, 1963. Paperback.

Montagu, Ashley, M. F. *Race, Science and Humanity.* Van Nostrand, 1963.

Myrdal, Gunner. *An American Dilemma.* 2 Vols. Reissue. McGraw-Hill, 1963. Paperback.

Noble, Jeanne. *Negro Women College Graduates.* Columbia, 1956.

Owens, William A. *Black Mutiny* (original title *Slave Mutiny*). Pilgrim, 1968. Paperback.

Parsons, Talcott, ed. *The Negro American* (Daedalus). Houghton-Mifflin, 1967. Paperback.

Pettigrew, Thomas F. *A Profile of the Negro American.* Van Nostrand, 1964.

Quarles, Benjamin. *The Negro in the Making of America.* Macmillan, 1964. Paperback.

Salk, Erwin. *A Layman's Guide to Negro History.* New, enlarged edition. McGraw-Hill, 1967.

Welsch, Erwin K. *The Negro in the United States: A Research Guide.* Indiana, 1965.

11

Christmas
December 25th

To say the least, Christmas "isn't what it used to be." The Christmas of trees, presents, prayers, cards, feasts, songs, and a time of gathering with family, friends, and loved ones is still very much with us. However, there are other serious challenges, penetrating attacks and legal decisions that affect how the school can or may honor the holiday in the public school setting.

The headlines in leading newspapers throughout the country reflect the times. For example, news stories with headlines such as the following reflects the mood, the thinking, the concerns and the tensions of our decade:

The Jesus Movement Spreading on Campus—A new interest in religion, which in some ways resembles the rise of radicalism in the late 1960's, is taking root on many of the nation's recently becalmed college campuses.

Two Life Styles Collide in Holiday Tragedy—Without Christmas they probably never would have met, for although they lived just a few miles apart for most of their lives, they also lived at opposite ends of the world. "One" was white and from the suburbs and a success at 36; "one" was black and from the city and, even at 21 years of age, unsuccessful. Another time, another place, they might have passed without noticing each other's families, for between them there were seven young children. But the two did meet, tragically, in a department store's Santa Claus line. When the encounter was over, "one" was dead of stab wounds and "one" was charged with murder.

All Is Calm, All Is Bright As the City Marks Holiday— Christmas means Rockefeller Center tree to some, and prayer, song, and reflection to others in the city.

The complexities of pressure groups, legal interpretations and a common desire to celebrate on an impartial, sincere and honest basis lends anxious moments to the dedicated classroom teacher. This chapter will explore a number of possibilities for creative teaching dealing with the theme of Christmas.

PERTINENT FACTS

1. The celebration of Christmas originated in the fourth century A.D., when the Church christianized a Roman feast associated with the winter solstice.
2. It is celebrated that in a humble state in the faraway city of Bethlehem, a baby was born some 1900 years ago. That baby was to save the world from sin. The birth of Jesus Christ is commemorated on December 25th.
3. In the Old Testament, the prophet Isaiah told of God's prophecy to Ahaz, the son of the King of Judah, that: "The Lord himself shall give you a sign. Behold, a virgin shall conceive and bear a son, and shall call his name Immanuel."
4. In the New Testament, it is written that Joseph and Mary, the father and mother of Jesus, after their arduous trip to Bethlehem were forced to spend the night in the manger.
5. The shepherds and the Three Wise Men who were led to Bethlehem by a bright star became the first worshipers of Jesus Christ.
6. The image of Santa Claus as we recognize him today was created by the great American cartoonist, Thomas Nast, in 1862.

SUGGESTED CLASSROOM ACTIVITIES

1. Once again there are numerous articles that may be drawn from local and national newspapers. In these papers one may find the scenes, the songs, the commentaries, the debates, and the "seeds" for providing students with a balance of materials showing how many ethnic groups celebrate the holiday season and the thinking and concerns of other peoples and groups.
2. Create a theme-centered multi-religious bulletin board.
3. Provide art posters and displays of Christmas themes.
4. Small skits and an assembly program for other grades.
5. Individual tasks and displays.
6. Reading plays and poems to ascertain the spirit and message in each.
7. Stories that are appropriate can be left open-ended. Pupils can then supply their own endings.
8. The use of the tape recorder for recitations or debates can make for an interesting classroom activity.
9. A vocabulary of Christmas can be developed.
10. An imaginary radio broadcast can be projected from the North Pole.

LESSON PLANS FOR
FRENCH CLASS AT CHRISTMASTIME
WITH MULTI-DISCIPLINE INVOLVEMENT

Purpose: To familiarize pupils with the French way of life by experiencing some French customs during the Christmas season.

Lesson Number One

An explanation of differences between the celebration of Christmas in the United States and in France.

Examples:
1. Less commercial (not so much emphasis on gift-giving)
2. December 25 is a religious day and a time for visiting friends and relatives

3. Gifts usually exchanged on the Epiphany (because this is the day when the three Magi arrived with their gifts)
4. Adults usually do not exchange gifts
5. Show differences between our conception of Santa Claus and the French Père Noël.

Lesson Number Two

Listen to some French Christmas carols and some that students are already familiar with. Hand out dittos of songs chosen for listening and have class sing them. In addition to the music covered in French class, pupils in music class could very well be doing a unit on Christmas around the world.

At the end of the lesson, pupils should be asked to give their impressions of Christmas in France through original sketches.

Lesson Number Three

Hand out a ditto of a simple French play, which the teacher can provide or which the pupils can write. This whole class would be devoted to choosing a cast of characters and other staff for the presentation and rehearsal. Pupils should be aided insofar as pronunciation is concerned and in any other details that may arise, but they should be responsible for the major part of the presentation of the play.

Lesson Number Four

Time should be devoted to rehearsing their play and working out the details. In art classes the sketches should be finished. In math classes, pupils could make geometric figures to be used for decorations in French class. Geometric designs are to be taken home and decorated.

The play should be recorded on tape in order that pupils may analyze their work.

Lesson Number Five

Pupils from other French classes could be invited to join the class for celebration of Epiphany and would be an audience for the play.

The room should be decorated with sketches and designs, and songs could be sung and listened to on a phonograph. A typical French snack of cheese, fruit and "grape juice" would add atmosphere to this lesson.

LESSON PLANS FOR SOCIAL STUDIES

This unit will permit pupils to examine their own and others' views concerning the relevance of the Christmas holiday, through the use of teamwork and creativity in producing a play. A major question should be: How meaningful is Christmas today to you and others (open choice) in the light of current social changes?

Activities

The class will be split into four "theatrical companies," each group occupying a corner of the room. Four leaders in the room will be chosen as directors.

Each group will retire to a corner and the director will hold elections or will choose a script writer, prop man, wardrobe mistress, and any other necessary officers.

Also, each group might decide on a name for their company. Each company will discuss such questions as: In the light of today's beliefs, is the celebration of Christmas relevant? Does it mean anything to the average person? If God is truly dead, why celebrate His son's birth? Has it lost its appeal because of commercialism? Are we not celebrating it just because our forefathers did?

During the discussions the script writer might take down the points that are brought up during the discussion and turn a copy in to the teacher with the name of the "theatrical company," along with the names of the officers and cast.

An outline of a play, and the story line to be followed will be completed by each group. This will be based on the discussion of the questions that were given earlier.

LESSON PLANS FOR THE STUDY OF MAJOR WORLD RELIGIONS

This study is intended to introduce pupils to the principal religions of the world.

Activities

1. On the bulletin board, have pictures that relate to the different major world religions.
2. Show a film on the major religions of the world.
3. Raise the question and discuss: What is Religion?
4. Arrange for speakers on the various world religions.
5. Give an outline of the major tenets of the principal religions to the class.
6. Allow students to choose a religion on which to give a written and/or oral report.
7. Have committees investigate possible sources of information. The first goal might be a bibliography of materials. Some possible sources of materials would be (a) school library, (b) class texts, (c) Readers' Guide to Periodical Literature, and (d) nearby college library.
8. Collect and show pictures of the followers of major world religions.
9. Have pupils give reports on major ideas of world religions.
10. Visit places of worship of the major faiths.

BIBLIOGRAPHY AND RESOURCE MATERIALS

Plays:

The Goblin at the Grocer's, by Delle Oglesbee Ross
The On and Off of a Christmas Gift, by Lettie C. VanDerveer
The Spirit of the Day, by Grace Torrey
What the Camels Brought to Mister Claus, by Mary Stewart Shelton (puppets)
The Blind Boy of Bethlehem, by Katherine Lee Bates

Poems:

"Before Dawn," by Walter de la Mare
"Now Every Child," by Eleanor Farjeon
"What If," by Robert Haven Schauffler
"A Christmas Carol," by Gilbert K. Chesterton
"At Christmas," by Edith Lovejoy Pierce
"Christmas," by Ernest Crosby
"Childhood Christmas," by Nancy Byrd Turner
"Christmas," by Bliss Carman
"I'm Wishing the Whole World Christmas," by Annette Wynne
"In the Manger," by Una A. Harsen
"On a Self-Portrait by Rembrandt," by Robert Haven Schauffler
"The Gifts," by Odell Shepard
"Aged Four," by Mildred Focht
"Yuletide Fires," (Old song)
"The Sending of the Magi," by Bliss Carman
"The Trapper's Christmas Eve," by Robert W. Service
"A Little Christmas Basket," by Paul Laurence Dunbar
"The Rann of the Christmas Tree," by Mary Frances Martin
"Joseph to Mary," by Sara Henderson Hay
"One Romance," by Theodore Watts-Dunton
"Christmas Candle," by Katherine Edelman
"Three Christmas Poems," by Robert Haven Schauffler
"Christmas Packages," by Wilfred Funk
"Six Green Singers," by Eleanor Farjeon
"The Thorn," by Mary Sinton Leitch
"The Three Kings' Road," by Anna Blake Mezquida

"The Swordless Christ," by John Richard Moreland
"The Voice of Christmas," by Harry Kemp
"The Storke (A Christmas Ballad)," King Edward VI's Prayer-book
"A Christmas Sonnet," by Robert Haven Schauffler
"Christmas 'Good-Night'," by Ethel Robb
"Christmas Trees," by Irene Wilde
"The Wise Men From the East," by Bliss Carman
"To a Snowflake," by Francis Thompson
"Southern Cross," by Leonora Speyer
"Christmas Carol," by Helene Mullens
"The Christmas Star," by Nancy Byrd Turner
"Babushka," by Edith M. Thomas
"Bethlehem of Judaea," (author unknown)
"Of Christmas," by Grace L. Schauffler
"The Foolish Fir Tree," by Henry Van Dyke
"The Twelve Days of Christmas," (Old English carol)
"To a Christmas Tree," by Mona Dale
"Santa Claus," by Leigh Hanes
"Harrowing Reflections," by Julia Boynton Green

Essays:

"Nothing Ever Happens," by Velma West Sykes
"Christmas Conservation," by Virginia Scott Miner
"The Palace and the Stable," by Hendrik Willem Van Loon
"Christmas," by Dorothy Canfield Fisher
"Share Your Christmas," by Mrs. Thomas A. Edison
"I Wish You All a Merry Christmas," by Jean Austin
"The Spirit of Giving," by Anne Bryan McCall
"The Heart of Christmas," by Henry C. Link
"Keeping Christmas," by Willard L. Sperry
"Signs, Symbols and Psychology," by Anne Bryan McCall
"Lighting the Yule Log," (*Literary Digest,* December 26, 1931)
"The Day Before," by Mary Lindsay Hoffman

Stories:

"The Boy in Nazareth," by Emile E. King
"Christmas Adventure," by Edith Mason Armstrong

"The Dolls' Christmas Tree," by Rebecca Deming Moore

"Primary Stories for Christmas Time," by Juanita Cunningham

"A Gift for Santa Claus," by Theda Pearson Hedden

"A Christmas Carol," by Charles Dickens

Films—Comparative Religions:

"Four Religions" (28 min.)—Makes a graphic comparison of the religious practices of Hindus, Buddhists, Muslims, and Christians.

"Great Religions" (16 min.)—Explores the origin of Buddhism and regional differences in form of the faith.

"Great Religions"—Islam. Photographed in many countries that know or have known the strength of Islam.

"Eye-witness No. 86"—Bar Mitzvah. Portrayal of ceremonies in which a Jewish youth confirms his faith. Follows several years of study of Hebrew language, scriptures, and customs.

"Three Great Religions"—Presents Taoism, Buddhism, and Confucianism.

Filmstrips—Comparative Religions:

"Christianity," Life, 1956 (90 frames, color).

"Buddhism," Life, 1956 (74 frames).

"Confucianism," Life, 1956 (67 frames).

"Hinduism," Life series (82 frames).

"Islam," Life series (82 frames).

"Judaism," Life series (75 frames).

"Dawn of Religion," Life (59 frames).

"The Early Christians," Life (79 frames).

"Hinduism" Avignette series (75 frames). Sheikh Publishing Co.

12

Chanukah and Passover

There has been a need for and a growing awareness of the lack of an understanding of religious beliefs and practices as a cultural force within societies of the world. In most instances, school curricula avoid this area because it is considered controversial. Yet, we need only to look about us at the obvious discontentment and apparent disillusionment of youth and their repeated requests for relevance within curricula to realize that understanding world religions is important and can help establish group identity.

Consider, then, a suggested unit for study that will (1) present an overview of World's Great Religions adaptable for use with any (or all) of the religions and, (2) a specific use of the overview to gain insight into the religion of Judaism. Why "Judaism"?

Within each month of an academic year, certain situations exist wherein differences of "life-styles" are apparent. Americans are prepared for the November observance of Thanksgiving and it is officially established and designed within the calendar. Just prior to that, however, some students may be absent because of a religious observance of a Harvest Festival, which is a "Jewish Thanksgiving," the Sukkoth.

In December, the spirit of and traditional preparations for the time of love, brotherhood, and good will toward men are overwhelmingly present. Through the progression of activities of this holiday time within the framework of the Christian culture, a holiday is observed by members of the Judaic culture called Chanukah, or Festival of Lights. In the different aspects of religious observances during this month, children, quite early in life, begin to be aware that friends, neighbors, sometimes even relatives, do not all believe or observe in like manner, and they wonder "why."

In March or April, again a similar situation exists. This is the time of "Easter" for Christians and of "The Passover" for Jews.

A unit of study based upon awareness of man's religions will hopefully provide a fresh perspective of, and an insight into, man and his culture. For those who cannot give time to a full study of Judaism, here are some versions that may prove to be helpful.

PERTINENT INFORMATION

Chanukah, the Festival of Lights, is observed for eight nights. Jews around the world begin celebrations at sundown (really the start of a new day). Chanukah recalls the time (168–165 B.C.) when a rustic guerilla band led by Judah Maccabee fought against the huge, superior Syrian army, which tried to impose a state religion on all people. Many groups submitted to the state and worshiped their ruler and their idols; but the stubborn little group of followers of monotheistic belief (in one God, a spiritual God of Judaism) refused to "bow down," or worship idols. The fight lasted three years and saved Judaism (the "mother religion" of Christianity and Islam) from being wiped out of existence.

At the time the resistance occurred, the Syrian Empire had spread over the entire Middle East, and the King of Syria ordered the extermination of all vestiges of Judaism so that subjected people would be "one people" worshipping the state pantheon of pagan gods.

"Whoever refuses should be put to death," it was decreed. Thousands of Jews were slain. Scripture scrolls were torn up and burned. Observance of the Sabbath was forbidden. A statue of the idol Jupiter was set up in the Jerusalem temple. Pagan altars were erected all over Israel, and patrols were deployed to force villagers to bow to the new "gods." But the Jews, led by Mattatias, refused to kneel and instead attacked the Syrian commander and killed him.

Mattatias and his sons fled to the Hills of Galilee, collecting a small army of guerilla fighters. Their continuing, relentless struggle marked the first successful use of guerilla tactics—lightning strikes, ambushes, night raids, harassment.

In the final battle, the little army (approximately 3,000) routed a Syrian force estimated at about 47,000.

It was a turning point in civilization, preserving a belief in one God that has spread around the earth. "The Maccabees"[1] became the first successful fighters for freedom of conscience. Their struggle was laden with universal implications.

After routing the Syrians, the Jewish people set about to cleanse and purify the temple for rededication to God. This gives the name to the holiday, for "Chanukah" means "dedication."

Legend says there was only enough holy oil to keep the Eternal Light before the Holy Ark burning for one day, but miraculously it continued to burn for eight days (and nights) until more holy oil could be prepared for use in the temple.

In observing the holiday, Jewish families use the symbolic eight-branched candelabra called a Menorah. One candle is lighted on the first night, and an additional candle is lighted on successive nights until, on the final night, eight small, colorful tapers glow in each menorah.[2]

Jews believe that the observance is relevant to recall their victory for the principle of religious freedom, and that it "assumes greater relevance in each passing year."

Chanukah is a happy holiday. In modern times it is celebrated by "rededicating oneself to ideals of the faith." Small gifts are given, especially to the children, on each of the eight nights. "Latkes," a kind of pancake made of potato mixture, are traditional at Chanukah parties, and children play a game called "dreydel." The dreydel is a small four-sided top inscribed with four Hebrew letters, which begin the words: "Nes Gadol Haya Sham," meaning "a great miracle happened here."

The game is one of "put and take." Children use nuts, candies, etc., and each participant puts one into the "pot." Then they take turns spinning the dreydel. If it comes up "N," the player gets nothing from the pot; "G" he takes all; "H" he takes half; "SH" he puts one in.

---

[1] Maccabee means "hammer" and Judah and his group were called Maccabees because they "hammered" away at the enemy's flanks.

[2] There are actually nine places for candles: eight for the eight nights the oil is believed to have lasted, and one for the placement of the "shamos" (or caretaker), which is used to light the other candles.

Sometimes coins are distributed to the children. Symbolic chocolate discs wrapped in gold or silver foil in little "money sacks" are also part of the holiday. Songs are sung, such as "Dreydel, Dreydel" and "Rock of Ages." Children role-play, taking parts of the Maccabees against the Syrians, similar to "Cops vs. Robbers," "Good Guys vs. Bad Guys," etc., with the outcome always known, of course, to end up happily!

Because Chanukah symbolizes the triumph of faith in God over brute force, it has long been a source of inspiration to the small and weak in number, who fight for liberty and justice against stronger tyrannical foes. It strengthens the conviction that religious freedom is everyone's right.

SUGGESTED ACTIVITIES

A. What is Religion?

Students should be asked to respond to this question in a general manner, to give a personal definition, and to define it according to the dictionary. In so doing, a wide range of answers and understanding or misunderstanding will become apparent. The teacher will need an awareness of the class (or group structure) in order to select relevant responses to the question.

Responses selected should attempt to lead the way into these areas: Religion (any) answers questions for people, i.e., it can help with "Why do I exist?" "What is true and real?" "How did the universe begin?" "Why do things happen the way they do?" "How does life end?" "Is there immortality?" "What is right and wrong?" "What is the good life?" (or any other questions considered relevant and/or pertinent).

B. Why is it important to study about religions?

Using the techniques used in "A," responses can then be selected to indicate that the study of religions is important because religion is part of all cultures, and of all history, and a study of it helps us to (1) understand differences between nations and cultures (both political and philosophical); (2) see similarities in views of the world by all humans; (3) appreciate our own beliefs by seeing them alongside those of others; (4) relate our religion to others in terms of origin, antiquity, source, beliefs, historicity, etc.; (5) keep from being "superior" in our own point of view, which leads to feelings of hostility; (6) work for ecumenism via a meaningful exchange of ideas between religious groups.

Although there are hundreds of different religions in the world, major ones for consideration might be Hinduism, Buddhism, Taoism, Confucianism, Shintoism, Judaism, Christianity, and Islam.

For purposes of student guidance in study or research, consider the following guide:

> When you read, or listen to class lectures and/or discussions or watch a film or filmstrip, you should try to identify these answers to the following questions.
>
> 1. What is faith called? (Name)
> 2. Is there a "founder"? If so, know name of person (or circumstances if there is no person given credit.)
> 3. Where in the world (geographically) did it begin? Spread to?
> 4. When did it begin (time period, or century, B.C., A.D., A.H., B.C.E.)?
> 5. Monotheistic or polytheistic faith? Name of God(s)?
> 6. Are there Holy Books, Scriptures, etc., used and/or followed by members of the faith?
> 7. Language of prayers, scriptures, people?
> 8. What do the people believe? Ways of worship; ceremony to become member of faith?
> 9. Name given to place of worship?
> 10. Leaders, prophets, apostles, etc.?
> 11. Important places, cities, rivers, buildings?
> 12. Special occasions (holidays, holy days of obligation, festivals)?

Activities

1. Examine symbols of Chanukah, such as Menorah, dreydel, etc.
2. Learn games of Chanukah.
3. Learn songs of Chanukah.

4. Draw mural depicting The Maccabees vs. The Syrians.
5. Draw the "Great Temple at Jerusalem" of the Ancient Jews.

PASSOVER [3]

PERTINENT INFORMATION

Passover, a Judaic holiday that occurs in early springtime (usually late March or early-to-mid-April) is a festival of freedom. It becomes significant for student understanding because it usually occurs at a time close to the Christian holidays of Palm Sunday, Good Friday (a legally observed holiday in many states, and in school systems) and Easter. The "Last Supper" of Christianity was actually a Passover Seder held in the Holy Land and observed by Jesus and His disciples.

Passover tells the story of the emancipation of Jews who were living in Egypt thousands of years ago (approximately 2,500 years ago). The "Seder" is a worship service as well as a festive meal. "Seder" means "order," so the order of the service carries out the recollection of the servitude of Jews under Pharoah, and their escape to freedom under the direction of Moses. The story is contained in the "Haggadah," the ancient book that tells the story. "Haggadah" is the Hebrew word for "telling" and the Passover Seder (order of service) is based on the Biblical direction (Exodus 13:8), "Thou shalt tell thy son in that day, saying, 'It is because of that which the Lord did for me when I came forth out of Egypt.' "

Passover is an eight-day holiday for Orthodox and Conservative Jewry, with Seders observed on the first and second nights. Reform Judaism observes a seven-day holiday, with a Seder on the first night of Passover.

The Seder is important to the entire household. Family members (as well as friends and/or guests) gather from afar, and it is customary to share this occasion with those who cannot get to their own home for this observance.

---

[3] The name is derived from the last of the ten plagues, in which God smote the eldest son of each household (of the Egyptians) but "passed over" the households of the Israelites, marked with the blood of a sacrificial lamb.

Children play a very important part in the Seder. The youngest son (or child) asks the traditional "four questions" in Hebrew, if possible. The "Ma Nishtanah" asks, "Why is this night different from all other nights?" The answers given by the father (or Seder leader) to the youngest son (or child) relates the drama of the Exodus of Moses and the Israelites from bondage of slavery under the cruel Pharoah of Egypt.

Special foods, prayers and songs help to recall the life of the forefathers and to maintain interest in the Jewish heritage.

Seder Plate contains:

Unleavened *matzoth*—representing the bread that Jews prepared in their haste when they did not have time to let the dough rise.

Maror (Bitter Herbs)—a reminder of slavery.

Haroseth—a mixture of apples, nuts, spices, wine (or grape juice) representing the mortar with which the Jews made bricks when they were slaves in the land of Pharoah.

The *shank bone of a lamb*—a reminder of paschal lambs that were used as sacrifice in the Temple of Jerusalem of early Judaism (in place of human sacrifice as was done by pagans).

A *roasted egg*—a symbol of a free will offering that usually was given at the sacrifice of a paschal lamb.

Parsley (or watercress)—a reminder of the continual rebirth of growing things.

Wine—a part of the ritual prayers and, during the recitation of the ten plagues visited by God upon the Egyptians, it is customary to dip (count off) into the wine ten times. Wine symbolizes happiness, and dipping off the droplets signifies that happiness is (was) incomplete and is an expression of sadness that some Egyptians had to suffer (by the plagues) before the Hebrews were freed from their enslavement and servitude.

The "Cup of Elijah" is a special cup (silver or crystal) or goblet of wine. Orthodox Judaism believes that "the prophet Elijah will foretell the coming of the Messiah," so by filling the cup with wine, Elijah's presence is anticipated at the Seder. It also is an expression of the hope that the "Age of the Messiah" (when all men will be at peace with each other and join the worship of the One God) will be fulfilled. (This hope for the Age of the Messiah is held by all branches of Judaism.)

Early in the service, a portion of one of the three matzoth, which are on the Seder plate of ceremonial foods, is hidden by the father. Children are given an opportunity to search for this part of the matzoth, called the "afikomen" (a Greek word meaning "dessert"). This adds to the joviality of the occasion as the finder is rewarded with a gift (or choice of a present) before returning the "'afikomen" to the dinner. The "afikomen" is eaten and is necessary to conclude the service. Once eaten, the food service is stopped. This is significant and helps to recall the ancient Hebrews who kept a small portion of the paschal sacrifice for the close of the meal. This practice was stopped when the Tenple was destroyed, and matzoth was substituted.

The father's use of a pillow, and reclining or relaxing rather than sitting erect is significant, because in ancient times a free man could eat in a relaxed manner, but slaves had to serve and eat in a hurry.

Passover helps all to remember that freedom needs to be guarded and held in high esteem, or it may be lost.

Activities

1. Examine symbols of The Passover, such as Seder Plate, Haggadah, etc.
2. Research food patterns of Orthodox Judaism (general food patterns) and also specific foods (restricted and/or permitted for The Passover).
3. Prepare a meal for a Passover Seder.
4. Participate in a Seder (or be invited to one).
5. Learn "four questions"—in English/Hebrew.
6. Learn songs of Passover.
7. Draw (or paint) mural, etc., of an ancient celebration of The Passover.

8. Draw (or paint) mural, etc., of a modern adaptation of The Passover.
9. Research background material of Egyptian culture and time of Judaic enslavement (pyramids, etc.).
10. Research background material of the time of Jesus, such as the "Last Supper."
11. Research modern beliefs of Christianity in relation to Palm Sunday, Maundy Thursday, Good Friday, Easter Sunday.

RESOURCES

The Children's Haggadah. Edited by Dr. A. M. Silbermann (translated from the Hebrew in Prose and Verse and with a Selection of Melodies). London: Shapiro, Valentine & Co., 1963. 5th edition.

Passover in Song and Story. Rabbi Charles Wengrove. New York: Shulsinger Bros. Pub. Co., 1960.

Living Heritage of Passover: With an Abridged Passover Haggadah in English. Edited by Solomon S. Bernards. #G 408 of Anti-Defamation League of B'nai B'rith Materials.

The Story Bible. Pearl S. Buck. Bartholomew House, Ltd. 1971.

One God: The Ways We Worship Him. Florence Mary Fitch. New York: Lathrop, Lee & Shepard & Co., 1944. (Printed by The Ullman Co., Inc., Brooklyn, N.Y.)

Augustus Caesar's World—B.C. 44—14 A.D. Genevieve Foster. New York: Chas. Scribner's Sons, 1947.

Your Neighbor Worships. Arthur Gilbert. New York: Friendly House Publishers.

Your Neighbor Celebrates. Arthur Gilbert and Oscar Tarcov. New York: Friendly House Publishers, 1957.

Teacher's Guide to Jews and Their Religion. Ruth Seldin. #B106 of Anti-Defamation League of B'nai B'rith Materials.

World's Great Religions (Special Edition for Young Readers). Editorial Staff of *Life* Magazine. New York: Golden Press, 1958.

The Living Heritage of Chanukah. David Greenberg and Solomon S. Bernards. Pamphlet #N528 of Anti-Defamation League of B'nai B'rith Materials, 315 Lexington Ave., New York, N.Y. 10016 or nearest A.D.L. Regional Office.

SECTION IV
INTERNATIONAL THEMES

13

United Nations Week
October

In this chapter there are pertinent facts that may be used to stimulate thought-provoking and interesting discussions among students. In addition, a series of carefully thought out and successfully used classroom activities are provided for evaluation and use. A typical lesson guide designed to illustrate many concrete and educationally sound methods of insuring student involvement is included. Finally, an annotated bibliography and a list of source materials will enhance the ability of the teacher to bring meaningful depth and breadth to youngsters while studying this topic.

PERTINENT FACTS

1. Official flag of the United Nations:

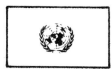

2. An official pledge to the United Nations flag does not exist.
3. Although many songs have been written about the United Nations, there is no official song or hymn.
4. The United Nations came into being on October 24, 1945.
5. The main deliberation organ of the United Nations is the Gen-

eral Assembly. The General Assembly represents all member states of the United Nations.

6. The Security Council is the organ on which member states have conferred primary responsibility for maintaining peace and security. There are fifteen members in the Security Council, five of which are permanent members, namely, The People's Republic of China, France, the U.S.S.R., the United Kingdom, and the United States of America.

7. The Economic and Social Council seeks to build a world of greater prosperity, stability and justice for all. This is the organ that organizes and coordinates all United Nations related agencies in the areas of economic and social work.

8. Trusteeship Council is the system for administration and supervision of territories, which are placed under the system by the General Assembly.

9. International Court of Justice is the judicial organ of the United Nations, which sits at The Hague in the Netherlands. It consists of fifteen judges elected by the Security Council and the General Assembly.

10. Secretariat is the administrative organ that services the other organs in administering the programs and policies laid down by them. Its head is the Secretary-General, who is appointed by the General Assembly on the recommendation of the Security Council.

11. Securing peace has been a prime goal of the United Nations since its inception. As an example, in 1965, the United Nations helped halt the fighting between India and Pakistan.

12. Disarmament has been another primary goal. Although the goal has not been attained to date, there have been hopeful signs such as the Treaty Banning Nuclear Weapons Tests in the Atmosphere, in Outer Space and Under the Water.

13. Atoms for Peace serves to encourage scientists to exchange information and work toward peaceful purposes.

14. Outer Space should be utilized for the benefits of mankind.

15. Under the United Nations Development Program, nearly 150 countries and territories are helped to build sound economies and to raise the living standards for all peoples.

16. UNICEF (United Nations Children's Fund) is currently aiding some 477 projects in 120 countries and territories. UNICEF was awarded the Nobel Peace Prize in 1965.
17. One of the main purposes of the United Nations is to promote and encourage respect for human rights.

SUGGESTED CLASSROOM ACTIVITIES

You may wish to try one or more of the following activities:

1. If possible, the class might visit the United Nations Headquarters in New York.
   a) Previsit study
   b) Points to look for
   c) Special individual topics to report on
   d) Follow-up activities.
2. Have the class make drawings, paintings, charts, representing U.N. ideas.
3. Show selected newspapers, magazines, etc., of U.N. subjects. Discuss the story involved.
4. Have the class prepare U.N. scrapbook.
5. Devise a class bulletin board of the U.N. in action.
6. Conduct a discussion based on the U.N. (structure, history, current events).
7. Have a skit, playlet or play on a U.N. subject written and produced by the students. May develop into an assembly program.
8. Invite a speaker to discuss the U.N. with the class or to speak at a U.N. assembly program. (This may create, however, a controversy in your community.)
9. Using an outline map of the world, show members and U.N. centers (New York City, Geneva, Paris, Rome, Washington, London, etc.).
10. Have students prepare a diagram of the flags of the U.N. members.
11. Have students write on U.N. themes, e.g., "Heroes of the U.N.," "Dag Hammarskjold," "U.N. Soldiers in Korea," "Katanga," "Middle East," "Vietnam."

12. Sing the song, "Happy Birthday, Dear United Nations." Prepare birthday cards of U.N.
13. Use U.N. films and filmstrips.
14. Have different groups select one U.N. country and explain its part in the U.N., and/or display some of their clothing, customs, traditions, etc.
15. Have the class attend a U.N. or foreign concert.
16. Have the class prepare a U.N. Day meal, in conjunction with a festival or fair.
17. Utilize A.F.S. exchange students in an assembly program.
18. Have the students prepare actual press releases for local newspapers.
19. Work with the librarian to establish a U.N. bookshelf.
20. Develop debates on current topics of the U.N.
21. Have children collect for UNICEF.

SUGGESTED LESSON GUIDES

Guideline I

1. Draw the symbol of the U.N. on an overlay transparency or on the chalkboard; have students respond to your projection.
   Typical kick-off questions:
   a) What is it?
   b) What does it stand for?
   c) Where is it located?
   d) How did it come into existence?
2. During a week in October, governors in some states proclaim this United Nations Week. Read the governor's proclamation.
   Typical questions:
   a) Why do you think the whole country observes United Nations Week?
   b) Why do you think the governor issued the proclamation?
   c) What does it really mean to you?
   d) Are there any words in the proclamation that we should examine?
3. Do you think we should observe or study something about the United Nations? If so, what?

4. We all agree that the U.N. plays a very important role in our lives. Therefore, what can we do to observe United Nations Week?
5. Would you like to plan a trip (if feasible; if not, an imaginary trip) to the U.N.?
6. What should we look for as we plan our trip to the U.N.?
7. Consider the following topics of interest:
   a) Countries of the United Nations
   b) Organs
   c) Issues
   d) Customs.
8. Give reasons why some people object to the U.N.

Guideline II

The United Nations is a most important world organization, and it is not only essential for students to develop an understanding of its origin and purpose, but it is also important to make them aware of its limitations in the world community. A realistic approach would be advisable if they are to understand the actual operation and capabilities of the U.N. Out of this study can also emerge many useful insights into the dynamics of human interaction on the various levels on which humans meet. The study of the U.N., therefore, can be a vehicle for understanding man in his culture and in his nature.

To illustrate how the theme, The United Nations, may be presented, consider the following lesson for a social studies class, which might cover about four days' study.

Day One:

To begin, in order to help students understand the origin of the United Nations, the teacher should write the following statement on the chalkboard: "The world has reduced in size in the past twenty-five years." Students should be asked to explain it. Different means of communication should be discussed, and the teacher should then ask if there is any way in which people can communicate better and avoid war. General discussion of the

United Nations organization should follow to find out what the students know.

Next, the teacher could introduce the topic of World War II and ask the names of Allied and Axis powers, outcome of the war, etc. The teacher could also sum up the general condition of the world toward the end of the war.

Ask the students if the world had ever known similar destruction previously. For example, how can we begin to appreciate the extent of the losses in human life and property? Students should discuss World War I and Woodrow Wilson's 14 Point Plan leading to the formation of the League of Nations. One might ask, for example, why it met with only partial success.

The teacher should describe the different bodies of which the United Nations is composed. These bodies are the General Assembly, Security Council, Economic and Social Council, Trusteeship Council, International Court of Justice, and the Secretariat. Students could also discuss the other educational and cultural organs with which they are familiar, such as UNESCO, WHO, FAO, etc.

For review, the teacher could ask students to name the different component bodies of the U.N. and their membership.

Assignment:

Students should be asked to select the one organ of the U.N. that they consider the most important and write a page on why they consider it important and what it has done to better the world up to now.

Plans for a field trip to the U.N., if feasible, can be planned here.

Day Two:

Purpose:

Students should take a critical look at the effectiveness of the U.N. as the peace keeper of the world.

The teacher could begin by asking questions about some of the more important organs of the U.N. that were covered the previous day. This help to focus the students' attention on the material to be completed. The teacher could then ask if the U.N. has been able to end all wars, and if not, why not? The teacher should ask about the U.N. peace-keeping successes. Emphasize the vital role the U.N. played in the Congo and in the Middle East.

Procedure:

The teacher may state, for instance: Today we are going to discuss the effectiveness of the United Nations as the peace keeper of the world.

The teacher should ask the students to name some of the most important problems that confront the world today. The list should include the following:

1. Vietnam War
2. Middle East Conflict
3. Arms race
4. Pollution
5. Overpopulation
6. Food shortages

The teacher could ask students why the U.N. has not been able to settle these and other problems. A discussion also of why the member countries often do not listen to the decisions of the U.N. may follow. Also, it should be pointed out that the U.N. has functioned successfully, and illustrations of its positive work should be given.

Review:

Some of the important problems faced by the U.N. and why they cannot be helped.

Assignment:

Write a brief description of what you consider a worthwhile U.N. goal and how it is being accomplished.

Day Three:

Purpose:

A field trip to the United Nations would allow students to see the General Assembly in session and gain firsthand knowledge of the workings of the U.N.

(Note: If a field trip is not feasible for reasons of travel, etc., an alternate activity could well be a trip to a consulate of a foreign government located in a capital city, or some other convenient area. One may also consider, for younger children, an imaginary trip.)

Introduction:

The teacher should hand out the fact sheet containing information about the U.N. tour, and the students should discuss and ask questions about it. For instance, it says that the site and money for the U.N. Plaza came from a John D. Rockefeller grant, but the land is considered not a part of the U.S. but belonging to the U.N., which has its own security force.

Procedure:

The group is met by a tour guide from Japan, who is dressed in a beautiful kimono. She says her name is Yoko Shimada. Evidently, she has spoken English for many years and the students have no trouble understanding her. The students are fascinated by her outfit and ask many questions about it.

Our first stop is the General Assembly where the Secretary General is addressing the session.

The huge auditorium has a head table where the Secretary General and the other officers sit; in the center of the room there is a table with secretaries taking notes. Behind the head table are three booths where the interpreters are located; there are four main languages used. Each delegate's seat is equipped with a headset.

The rest of the seats are arranged in a large semicircle facing the head table. The chief delegate sits in the first row and has three seats behind for his advisors.

Next, a tour of the Security Council conference room and offices of the Secretariat is conducted.

At lunch-time, the students eat boxed lunches in the lounge area.

After lunch, the students visit the International Art Gallery, children's art gallery, and the Delegates' Lounge, where they will meet some of the delegates from other countries.

Finally, the students visit the International Gift Shop. By this time it is 3:00 P.M., and time to return to school.

Assignment:

Students should be asked to write a paragraph on the aspect of the U.N. that impressed them most.

Announcement:

Bring in costumes to represent the various countries.

Day Four:

Purpose:

Use facts learned in the past three days to conduct a General Assembly.

Introduction:

The teacher should give students time to dress in their costumes to represent the different nations. The students should have brought in colored bedsheets, scarves, etc. They should then settle themselves in a semicircle and prepare to select the Secretary General.

The teacher might indicate that today we are going to conduct a meeting of the General Assembly of the United Nations to discuss the crisis in the Middle East.

After the Secretary General is selected, he makes some opening remarks and turns the floor over to the Arab delegate.

The Arab delegate says that Israel should return to the boundary lines prior to the recent war.

The delegate from Israel defends Israel's position by stating that the war was fairly fought and, thus, they have a right to the land.

The British delegate states that shipping has been seriously curtailed because of the Suez being closed.

The discussion goes back and forth without any agreement being reached.

A resolution to censure Israel for bombing some ports in Lebanon is voted on and passed.

Assignment:

Answer the question: From what has been learned during the week, why is the U.N. very limited in its effectiveness? Where has it been successful? How has its role changed since its origin?

BIBLIOGRAPHY AND RESOURCE MATERIALS

The First Twenty-five Years of the United Nations from San Francisco to the 1970's, by Dean Rusk. Bureau of Public Affairs, Department of State, Washington, D.C. Series S-No. 17.
> Text of the Dag Hammarskjold *Memorial Lecture, January 10, 1964. The U.N.—How the U.N. Was Set Up.*

Do You Know the Facts About UNESCO and UNICEF? American Association for the United Nations, 345 East 46th Street, New York, N.Y.
> Briefly stated facts to correct misstatements concerning UNESCO and UNICEF. 1962.

United Nations. Monthly Bulletins, Sales Section, N. Y.
> Provides full information on Sales Publishing programs; the Monthly List, and the full description of important titles.

You and the United Nations. Department of State, Superintendent of Documents, U.S. Government Printing Office, Washington, D.C. #7442. 25¢
> Answers the questions of U.S. citizens regarding the U.N. and its value.

Past-Present-Future of the U.N. by Adlai Stevenson. #21 Sidney Hillman Foundation, 15 Union Square, New York, N. Y.
> 1961 brief report by Adlai Stevenson.

United Nations Voting Blocs. American Observer, October 21, 1963. Civic Education Service, 1733 K Street, N.W., Washington, D.C.
> Readable Junior High School subscription.

A New United Nations Exhibit. United Nations, Sales Section, Public Service, New York, N.Y.
> A U.N. Publications Kit at $3.95 plus 50¢ handling charge.

United Nations Declaration on the Elimination of All Forms of Racial Discrimination. November, 1963. U.N. Office of Public Information, New York, N.Y.
> Eleven articles to promote respect and eliminate discrimination.

United Nations Day. U.S. Government Printing Office, 1964-0-742-390, Washington, D.C.
> Poster Proclamation.

The U.N. in Action. U.S. Committee for the United Nations, New York, N.Y.
> Discussion on U.N. in action and the U.S. position.

Facts for Fallacies. U.S. Committee for the U.N., 375 Park Avenue, New York, N.Y.

Peacekeeping Since 1946, by Betty Lall. Bulletin of Atomic Scientists, Foundation for Nuclear Science, Inc., 935 East 60th Street, Chicago, Illinois. May, 1964.

On disarmament issues.

Address List; Permanent Missions to the U.N. Bulletin #2, February, 1964. University of Bridgeport, Bridgeport, Conn.

Compiled for teachers wishing information and literature concerning foreign countries.

Information Services and Embassies in the U.N.—of Members of the U.N. U.N. Public Information Office, October, 1963, New York, N.Y.

Supplement to United Nations Books in Print 1961. United Nations, New York

U.N. Books, Flags and Maps. Sales Section, Publishing Service, New York.

Ranges from 50¢ to $1.50 for posters, charts; books to $6.00.

U.N. We Believe, Progress. Prepared by the Grand Union Company.

What you can do to help the U.N.

Everyman's U.N. U.N. Publishing Sales #59.1.2, $3.50.

A complete handbook of the functions and activities of the U.N. and its specialized agencies.

United Nation Periodicals. United Nations, New York, 1961.

Let's Look at the Record. American Association for the U.N., 345 East 46th Street, New York, N.Y. 1961.

The Arrow Book of the U.N., by Dobler. Scholastic Book Service, New York, N.Y. 1963.

Answers boys' and girls' questions about the U.N.

Flags of the U.N. Barker Brothers, New York, N.Y.

The U.N. and How It Works, by David Coyle. Mentor Books, 501 Madison Avenue, New York, N.Y. 1960.

NEA—Materials to Help You Teach About the United Nations. 1201 Sixteenth Street, N.W., Washington, D.C.

Publications, films, filmstrips.

United Nations 16mm Film Catalogue. Office of Public Information, United Nations, New York.

Many excellent productions of U.N. in action.

From: *U.N. Sales Section,* New York:

a. U.N. Study Kit, $1.25. (Background materials for study and discussion.)

  b. U.N. Flag and Map Kit, $1.50. (Illustrated booklet on U.N. activities.)
  c. General Assembly of the U.N., 30¢. (Principal organ of the U.N.)
  d. *International Trusteeship System and the Trusteeship Council,* 30¢. (Explains trusteeship and council work.)
  e. *Economic and Social Council,* 30¢. (Activities in the economic and social field.)
  f. *Information Kit for Visitors to U.N. Headquarters,* 65¢. (What and how U.N. works.)
  g. *What It Is—How It Works—What It Does,* $3.50 per 100. (Leaflets.)
  h. *Technical Assistance in Brief,* $5.00 per 100.
  i. *United Nations in Brief,* $5.00 per 100.
From: *United Nations Bookshop.* General Assembly Building, New York, N.Y.
  a. Teaching and Study Guide List
  b. Economics
  c. World Bank
  d. Visuals
  e. For Younger Readers
  f. U.N. Information
  g. Yearbooks
  h. U.N. in Action
From: *Civic Leader,* Vol. 34, #3, September 21, 1964, Washington, D.C.
  a. Aids for U.N. Programs
  b. Posters and Displays
  c. Background Materials
  d. Resource Guides
  e. Bookshelf Selection

14
Earth Day (Ecology)
April 22

Contemporary youth is profoundly concerned about the environment. Its idealism and action has often resulted in meaningful pressure for environmental action—pressure upon political, educational, and industrial institutions. Earth Day is a symbol of the awareness of a problem that has been raised to the level of a national issue. Ecological disasters of the 1960's, and decades before, have caused us to reconsider some of the pessimistic predictions of twenty or thirty years ago. The death of Lake Erie, the wreck of the Torry Canyon, the Santa Barbara Oil Spill, and the extinction of many species of animal life should emphasize those imperatives resulting from the limited resources of our environment. The Connecticut Audubon Council summarized the problem as follows:

> Environment is suddenly a big issue. Politicians, bureaucrats, and businessmen are leaping to record themselves in favor of a cleaner environment. But the record of achievements is bleak. We have had too much rhetoric and too little understanding of ecological problems—while the crisis becomes steadily, perhaps irretrievably, worse. Something more is needed than a dose of American know-how: something more profound than sanitation is at stake. We boast of our affluence while we choke on our effluence. There is smog in Bridgeport, sewage in Long Island Sound, industrial pollu-

tion killing the Naugatuck River, DDT in our food, auto dumps all over our state, decay and litter in our cities and along our highways. We put a man on the moon, but we still put our garbage into our drinking water. Our cities are unlivable, and we are killing the countryside in the name of progress.[1]

Earth Day is a symbol of an ongoing commitment that must be shared by all of us. Of the many concerns facing us, none is more vital than the problem of our natural resources—pollution of air, water and soil, and the loss of living species and wildlife. The school is not alone in an overt expression of concern. This point is exemplified by an editorial in *Trial* magazine.

Since the beginnings of recorded history, there have been conflicts between man and man, and between man and the State. These early conflicts will continue, regardless of far and wide our penetration into space. If our bar association has been dedicated to one principle, it is that the common law system is the best system for resolving these conflicts.

The time has now arrived for using this system in resolving conflicts between man and his environment.[2]

PERTINENT FACTS

The roots of environmental concern rest in the early Conservation movements that influenced organizations and legislation. Some of these movements follow:

1. Early American leaders, Washington and Jefferson, were proponents of farming techniques that prevented soil erosion (contour plowing).
2. Henry Thoreau suggested the establishment of wilderness areas.
3. John J. Audubon created world-wide interest in birds.
4. George Perkins Marsh (1801-1882) wrote, "The Earth Is

---

[1] Connecticut Audubon Council, *Connecticut Newsletter*, Vol. 3, No. 10, April 11, 1970. Connecticut Audubon Council, Farmington, Conn.

[2] Published by the American Trial Lawyers Association, Cambridge, Mass. Vol. 5, No. 5, August/September, 1969, p. 8.

Modified by Human Action" in 1864. This helped to arouse world-wide interest in conservation.

5. 1872—Yellowstone National Park was established by the government.
6. 1872—Arbor Day was suggested by J. Sterling Morton.
7. 1891—Congress passed a law giving the president the right to establish forest reserves.
8. 1898—Gifford Pinchot became head of the Department of Agriculture, Division of Forestry.
9. 1905—Under Pinchot's leadership, the Division became the U.S. Forest Service.
10. 1908—President Theodore Roosevelt, an ardent conservationist, appointed Pinchot head of the National Conservationist Commission. President Roosevelt distinguished himself both as a conservationist and outdoorsman. Under his Administration, 125 million acres were added to national forest reserves.
11. 1909—The North American Conservation Conference was founded, including the U.S., Canada, Newfoundland, and Mexico.
12. 1909—The first major textbook on conservation was published by Charles R. Von Hise, *The Conservation of the National Resources of the United States*.
13. 1911—Congress passed Week's Law, an act to enlarge national forests.
14. 1916—The National Park Service was founded under the Wilson Administration.
15. 1916—Wilson signed the first Migratory Bird Treaty with Canada.
16. In the 1930's, the Roosevelt Administration sponsored numerous projects:
    The Civilian Conservation Corps
    The Tennessee Valley Authority
    The Soil Erosion Service (Dept. of the Interior)
    The Taylor Grazing Act
    The Flood Control Act of 1936.
17. 1954—The Watershed Protection and Flood Prevention Act

was passed.

18. 1955—A twenty-year program was begun by the Department of the Interior to restore federal grazing lands.

19. 1957—"Operation Outdoors" began a five-year program by the U.S. Forest Service, which improved national forest facilities.

SUGGESTED ACTIVITIES

Half-day or day-long Earth Days have been implemented in many schools. Typical of these was one that involved the students of the Fox Lane Middle School in Bedford, N. Y. in 1969. Activities included total student body involvement in the following:

1. Seminars and teach-ins conducted by students, teachers, and visitors from the community.

2. Planting of trees, flowers and shrubs by students. Money for the purchase of these was raised through previous bake sales, scrap drives, etc. Local nurseries, citizens and civic groups also made donations as a result of student canvassing.

3. Building of picnic tables and benches by students, for student use during lunch hours.

4. Removal of litter from school or community land.

5. Cleaning of ponds.

6. Publicity, and community awareness as a result of student activity. What about problems of urban centers? There have been successful workdays where groups of students have traveled into urban communities and participated in clean-up campaigns. Student-generated activity in this direction can provide a meaningful experience for both participants and recipients.

7. Leadership by student groups formed for the purpose of continuing concern (Concerned Conservationists Club).

An illustration of a total school commitment is the program developed by the Kathleen Laycock Country Day School of Greens Farms, Connecticut. A project, "Lemon Into Lemonade," was de-

veloped by Mr. Scholl, Director of Development, and is given below in anecdotal form:

LEMON INTO LEMONADE [3]

THE LEMON:	Dimly perceived rumblings of a day-long "Teach-in"; picketing; class boycott; all centered around "Earth Day"—latest target for Vietnam war protesters and similar types.
THE LEMONADE:	A day-long "Learn-in" for a K-12 school with follow-up activities on a short- and long-term basis. Improved relations with town and visiting schools.
DEFINING THE PROBLEM:	Beyond the knowledge that this day was planned by groups of older students to be based upon a protest against the pollution, littering, and destruction of our environment, not much was known about the form these protests would take when planning commenced. It was decided that early action would be required to get desirable speakers, displays and to coordinate activities. It was decided to centralize all planning in the hands of one faculty member, and this planning began about two months before the actual day. The planning steps in the order of their occurrence can roughly be grouped as follows:

1. Scheduling of school time for the day.
2. Tying down people who would be available for speaking during the day.

---

[3] Contributed by Robert P. Scholl, Westport, Conn.

3. Canvassing of state and regional agencies for suitable display material.
4. Contacting industries in the area for display material.
5. Organizing a very small nucleus of faculty members to advise, assemble material, and a few students to contribute time and effort also.
6. Arranging for publicity, invitations, poster contests, etc.
7. Planning the day itself and the follow-up activities on several grade and interest levels.
8. Involving the students and holding the day itself.
9. Distribution of material, writing of thank-you notes, and moving into evaluation and follow-up phase.

PLANNING FOR THE FIRST DAY: Without going into great detail, it may be seen from the attached material, including the program for the day, and samples of the material distributed to the students and the public, that a great many people were involved. The preceding paragraphs indicate the kind of planning that went into the production. At the time in March when State agencies were asked for material to be used in an ecological program, many of the people in the agencies looked completely blank at the first mention of the "Earth Day." By the time of the second visit in late March, almost everyone knew about some of the programs being planned, and all were inundated with requests for material. The same thing happened with the media. A highly successful, recorded panel discussion was arranged for with a local radio station far in advance of the day. There was little doubt that the radio station received many requests for coverage of other Earth Day activities thereafter, but they felt they were concentrating enough on the day in view of the three broadcasts they had already promised to make. The exposure to the community here was excellent. Much of the material received from State agencies was used to prepare bulletin boards on water pollution, air pollution, trash and garbage disposal and related subjects. A poster contest was held, with a first prize and an honorable mention awarded in each of the schools, lower, middle, and upper. Other touches included everything from hand-inscribed copies of the "Earth Day Handbook" presented to the panelists, to a pot of geraniums for the hard-working office staff who stayed late the night before Earth Day to turn out the final copy of the program. As the day approached, students began to take an interest. Advanced biology classes were asked to become guides to take members of the eighth grade of a school that had called us as a result of our advance publicity and asked if they could send some students over. This gave us the happy thought that we should invite middle school grades in two other schools, and one of them accepted and sent the entire seventh grade. This led to a further project of guiding the students both through the nearby seashore and through marshland, which belongs to the school.

FOLLOW-UP ACTIVITIES: Earth Day itself was a great success from the point of view of the school children. Two local public high school students had produced a sound and light show, featuring slides of some of the beauty and ugliness of our world; this was a smashing success. Students began to respond during the morning discussion, which, as can be seen from the program, included primarily people who were oriented in directions other than the immediate town area. By the afternoon discussion, composed of those who were primarily interested in action on the local level, the students were beginning to take a great interest in their role in preserving our environment. The day before Earth Day, the lower school had determined that its series of skits, which were to be presented only for the benefit of other lower school students, could be presented for the rest of the school and the public as well, provided they were held outside and due note was taken of their spontaneous and unrehearsed nature. These skits were a great success with the older students and visitors, and an idea of the verve with which these were executed can be surmised by imagining the "litter family" going on a picnic, being followed by "Tidy Tim" picking up behind them.

All of the material received from the state, regional and local agencies has been sent to the School Library for filing. Students have begun to inquire, and take out books on the suggested reading list. The students themselves have begun to react, without prodding or direction. For example, plans are now afoot to clean up the marshland, which the school owns —a constructive sign. Perhaps movies such as the "Long Tidal

River" and "Lassie's Litter Bit" shown in the film festival have helped.

Two other manifestations are evident and interesting. The first is the decision by several students that they would like to participate in some sort of Conservation Club next year. It is thought that this would take the form of an Outing Club, with students cleaning up park land, town-owned land, and private open space, perhaps planting trees obtained from the State of Connecticut to act as windbreaks, soil savers, and bird cover.

The second manifestation is the request for several senior projects in the study of ecology and pollution, and plans next year for a course in ecology for those interested. Conservation curriculum planning in the lower school is also underway.

RESOURCE MATERIALS

Brown, Harrison. *The Challenge of Man's Future.*
Carson, Rachel. *The Silent Spring.*
Carson, Rachel. *The Sea Around Us.*
Commoner. *Science and Survival.*
Dasmann, Raymond. *The Destruction of California.*
Daedalus. Fall, 1967 Issue.
Dubos, Rene. *So Human An Animal.*
Erlich, Paul. *The Population Bomb.*
Galbraith, John K. *The New Industrial State.*
Galbraith, John K. *The Affluent Society.*
Graham, Frank. *Disaster by Default: Politics and Water Pollution.*
Herber, Lewis. *Crisis in Our Cities.*
Keats, John. *The Insolent Chariots.*
Kormondy. *Principles of Ecology.*
League of Women Voters Education Fund. *The Big Water Fight.*
Leopold, Aldo. *A Sand County Almanac.*
Matthiessen. *Wildlife in America.*
McHarg, Ian L. *Design With Nature.*
Meyer, John Robert. *The Urban Transportation Problem.*
Mishan. *The Costs of Economic Growth.*
Muir, John. *My First Summer in the Sierra.*
Muir, John. *The Mountains of California.*
Mumford, Lewis. *The City in History.*
Mumford, Lewis. *The Urban Prospect.*
Nash. *Wilderness and the American Mind.*
Odum. *Ecology: The Subversive Science.*
Owens, Wilfred. *The Metropolitan Transportation Problem.*
Paddock, William and Paul. *Famine 1975: America's Decision, Who Will Survive.*
Schwartz, William. *Voices for the Wilderness.*
Thoreau, Henry. *Walden.*
Thoreau, Henry. *A Week on the Concord and Merrimack Rivers.*
Udall, Stewart. *The Quiet Crisis.*
Udall, Stewart. *1976: Agenda for Tomorrow.*
Whalen, Richard. *A City Destroying Itself.* (Air and water pollution)
Whyte. *The Last Landscape.*

Books on Conservation and Wildlife

Ashbaugh, Byron, and Beuschlein, Muriel. *Things To Do in Science and Conservation.* Danville, Illinois: Interstate Printers & Publishers, 1960.

Bates, Marston. *The Forest and the Sea.* New York: New American Library, 1961.

Bibliography of Conservation Books, Booklets, and Teaching Aids. Washington, D.C.: Government Printing Office.

Chase, Stuart. *Rich Land, Poor Land: A Study of Waste in Natural Resources.* New York: McGraw-Hill, 1934.

Conservation in American Schools. Washington, D.C.: National Education Association, American Association of School Administrators, 1951.

Concepts of Conservation. New York: Conservation Foundation, 1963.

Cornell Science Leaflets. Ithaca, N.Y.: Cornell University Press, 1946–52, Vol. 39, No. 4, *The Story of Conservation.*

Materials to Help Teach Forest Conservation. List of teaching aids. Washington, D.C.: U.S. Department of Agriculture, 1953.

Munzer, Martha E., and Brandwein, Paul F. *Teaching Science Through Conservation.* New York: McGraw-Hill, 1960.

Osborn, Fairfield. *Limits of the Earth.* Boston: Little, Brown, 1953.

Osborn, Fairfield. *Our Plundered Planet.* Boston: Little, Brown, 1952.

Pinney, Roy. *Vanishing Wildlife.* New York: Dodd, Mead, 1963. (Conservation of wildlife, extinct species, and conservation problems)

Basic Ecology Bibliography

Overview of Ecological Problems:

Borgstrum. *The Hungry Planet.* Collier-Macmillan.

Carson. *Silent Spring.* Crest, 1962.

Commoner. *Science and Survival.* Viking, 1967.

Ehrlich. *The Population Bomb.* Ballantine, 1968.

Leinwand. *Air and Water Pollution.* Washington Square Press, 1969.

Longgood. *Poisons in Your Food.* Pyramid, 1960.

Marine. *America the Raped.* Simon and Schuster, 1969.

Marx. *The Frail Ocean.* Ballantine/Sierra Club. 1967.

Paddock. *Famine 1975.* Little, Brown & Co.

Rienow and Train. *Moment in the Sun.* Ballantine/Sierra Club, 1967.

Rudd. *Pesticides and the Living Landscape.* University of Wisconsin Press.

Shurcliff. *SST and Sonic Boom Handbook*. Ballantine, 1970.

The Environmental Handbook. Ballantine. (Prepared especially for April 22 Teach-in.)

Texts and Anthologies:

Billings. *Plants and the Ecosystem*. Wadsworth.

Buchsbaum. *Basic Ecology*. Boxwood Press.

Carvajal and Munzer. *Conservation Education—A Selected Bibliography*. Interstate Printers, Danville, Illinois. (Elementary through high school.)

Cox, *Conservation Ecology*. Appleton-Century-Crofts.

Elton. *Ecology of Animals*. Barnes & Noble.

Kormandy. *Concepts of Ecology*. Prentice-Hall.

Odum. *Ecology*. Holt, Rinehart, Winston.

Shepard and McKinley. *The Subversive Science, Essays Toward an Ecology of Man*. Houghton-Mifflin.

Storer. *The Web of Life*. Signet.

The Human Animal:

Ardrey. *The Territorial Imperative*. Delta-Dell, 1966.

Dubos. *So Human an Animal*. Doubleday or Charles Scribner's Sons, 1969.

Galbraith. *The Affluent Society*. Mentor.

Michael. *The Unprepared Society*. Vintage, 1969.

Morris. *The Naked Ape*. Dell.

Snyder. *Earth Household*. New Directions.

Whole Earth Catalog. Portola Institute.

Environmental Film List:

"Air Pollution: Take a Deep Deadly Breath" (54 min., color). Contemporary. ABC Documentary.

"Beargrass Creek" (19 min., color). Stuart Finley. The poignant tragedy of a small tributary stream, its promising start, and its sad end due to pollution.

"Bulldozed America" (25 min., B/W). Carousel. Bulldozer and commercial interests tear apart countryside and turn it into supermarkets, highways, etc.

"By Land, Sea and Air" (31 min., color). Oil, Chemical, and Atomic Workers Int. Union. Effects of pesticides on farm workers and environment of California.

"Challenge to Mankind" (28 min., B/W). Contemporary. Five world experts speak of threat of overpopulation.

"Cities in Crisis" (22 min., color). Order #6812. Extension Media.
   Impressionistic film of urban sprawl and unplanned growth.
"Clean Waters" (20 min., color). Order #3972. Extension Media.
   Illustrates dangers of water pollution and shows proper sewage treat-
   ment.
"Crisis on Kanawha" (20 min., color). Stuart Finley. Shows sources of
   industrial water pollution and some methods of eliminating it.
"A Day at the Dump" (15 min., color). Free. Environmental Control
   Administration. Story of Kenilworth Dump in Washington, D.C. and
   its planned conversion to a public park.
"The Everglades: Conserving a Balanced Community" (11 min., color).
   Britannica.
"First Mile Up" (28 min., B/W). Contemporary. Problems of air pol-
   lution and its effect on human health. Toronto and Los Angeles as
   examples.
"For All to Enjoy" (20 min., color). Conservation Foundation. Satirical
   approach to uncontrolled development in National Parks.
"Green City" (23 min., color). Stuart Finley. Civic action to preserve
   green space and open space as cities grow.
"Man and His Resources" (28 min., B/W). Contemporary.
"A Matter of Time" (27 min., color). Conservation Foundation. Historical approach to environmental deterioration.
"Megapolis: Cradle of the Future" (22 min., B/W). Britannica. Dynam-
   ics of urbanization and emphasis on need for careful planning.

Index

A

Abernathy, Dr. Ralph, 147
Adams, John, 19, 20, 23, 24
Adams, Samuel, 20
Amendments to Constitution, 70–76
American Bible Society, 88
American Indians, 87–88, 151–152
American Legion, 65
   Know Your America, 23n, 27, 41–46
   Memorial Day celebrations, 56
   National Americanism Commission, 41
American Revolution, 19–21, 34, 147
American Trial Lawyers Association, 134
Amerson, Lucius A., 146
Anderson, Marian, 141
Andros, Sir Edmund, 33
Arbor Day, 195
Arlington National Cemetery, 50
Armistice Day, 49 (*See also* Veterans Day)
Art displays:
   Black America Week, 130
   Christmas, 162
   Memorial Day, 57, 64
   United Nations Week, 181
Articles of Confederation, 80
Atoms for Peace, 182
Attucks, Crispus, 147
Audio-visual aids:
   Lincoln's Birthday, 118
   Memorial Day, 61–63
Audubon, John J., 194

B

Benedict, Dr. Ruth, 150
Berkeley settlement in Virginia, 89
Bill of Rights, 25, 70, 74–75
   ratification of, 74

Birmingham (Alabama) civil rights demonstration, 143
Black Americans:
   art displays, 130
   contributions of, 137
   progress (1941–71), 138–147
   role in United States history, 147–148
Black History Week, 137–158
   bibliography, 157–158
   classroom activities, 148–149
   leading Blacks, 147–148
   progress of Black Americans, 138–147
Black Muslims, 144
Black Nationalism, 144
'Black Power" movement, 146
"Blowin' in the Wind," 61–63
Booth, John Wilkes, 115
Boston Tea Party, 20, 34
Boudinot, Elias, 88
Bradford, Governor William, 89
Brooke, Senator Edward, 147
Brooks, Gwendolyn, 140
Brotherhood, 148
Brown vs. Board of Education, 141, 151
Buddhism, 173
Bulletin board displays, 56
Bunche, Ralph J., 140, 142
Bunker Hill, 34

C

Cabot, John, 33
Calhoun, John, 26
Canadian Remembrance Day, 49
Carmichael, Stokely, 146
Cartier, Jacques, 33
Cartoons, 104
   political, 78
Case, Andrew, 57;i
Catholic minorities, 150
Chanukah, 169–174, 178
   classroom activities, 172–174